PRINCIPLES OF
COMMUNITY ENGAGEMENT
SECOND EDITION

**Clinical and Translational Science Awards Consortium
Community Engagement Key Function Committee Task
Force on the Principles of Community Engagement**

NIH Publication No. 11-7782
Printed June 2011

For sale by the Superintendent of Documents, U.S. Government Printing Office
Internet: bookstore.gpo.gov   Phone: toll free (866) 512-1800;   DC area (202) 512-1800
Fax: (202) 512-2104 Mail: Stop IDCC, Washington, DC 20402-0001

ISBN 978-0-16-088803-8

TABLE OF CONTENTS

CTSA Community Engagement Key Function Committee Task Force on the *Principles of Community Engagement* (Second Edition)

Donna Jo McCloskey, RN, PhD, National Center for Research Resources, NIH (Chair)

Sergio Aguilar-Gaxiola, MD, PhD, University of California, Davis (Co-Chair)

J. Lloyd Michener, MD, Duke University (Co-Chair)

Tabia Henry Akintobi, PhD, MPH, Morehouse School of Medicine

Ann Bonham, PhD, Association of American Medical Colleges

Jennifer Cook, MPH, Duke University

Tamera Coyne-Beasley, MD, MPH, University of North Carolina at Chapel Hill

Ann Dozier, PhD, University of Rochester School of Medicine and Dentistry

Robert Duffy, MPH, University of California, Davis

Milton (Mickey) Eder, PhD, University of Chicago, Access Community Health Network

Paul Fishman, PhD, University of Washington

Jo Anne Grunbaum, EdD, Centers for Disease Control and Prevention

Sheila Gutter, PhD, Weill Cornell Medical College

Karen Hacker, MD, MPH, Harvard University

Michael Hatcher, DrPH, Agency for Toxic Substances and Disease Registry

Suzanne Heurtin-Roberts, PhD, MSW, National Cancer Institute, NIH

Mark Hornbrook, MD, Kaiser Permanente Center for Health Research

Shantrice Jones, MPH, Centers for Disease Control and Prevention

Michelle Lyn, MBA, MHA, Duke University

Mary Anne McDonald, DrPH, MA, Duke University

David Meyers, MD, Agency for Healthcare Research and Quality

Barbara Moquin, PhD, APRN, National Center for Complementary and Alternative Medicine, NIH

Patricia Mullan, PhD, University of Michigan

Nancy Murray, DrPH, MA, University of Texas Health Science Center at Houston

Ruby Neville, MSW, Substance Abuse and Mental Health Services Administration

Cheryl Perry, PhD, University of Alabama at Birmingham

Dana Sampson, MS, MBA, Office of Behavioral and Social Sciences Research, NIH

Mina Silberberg, PhD, Duke University

Meryl Sufian, PhD, National Center for Research Resources, NIH

Stephen Updegrove, MD, MPH, Yale University

David Warner, MD, Mayo Clinic

Charlene Raye Weir, RN, PhD, University of Utah

Sharrice White-Cooper, MPH, Centers for Disease Control and Prevention

Editorial and Research Staff

Mina Silberberg, PhD, Duke University (Chair)

Jennifer Cook, MPH, Duke University

Cheryl Drescher, BEd, Duke University

Donna Jo McCloskey, RN, PhD, National Center for Research
  Resources, NIH

Sarah Weaver, MPH, Duke University

Linda Ziegahn, PhD, University of California, Davis

External Reviewers

Barbara Alving, MD, FCCP, National Center for Research Resources, NIH

Ahmed Calvo, MD, MPH, Health Resources and Services Administration

Teresa Cullen, MD, MS, Indian Health Service

William Elwood, PhD, Office of Behavioral and Social Sciences
  Research, NIH

Carol Ferrans, PhD, RN, FAAN, University of Illinois at Chicago

Sarah Greene, MPH, University of Washington

Thelma Hurd, MD, University of Texas Health Science Center
  at San Antonio

Laurel Leslie, MD, MPH, Tufts University

Leandris Liburd, MPH, PhD, Centers for Disease Control and Prevention

Doriane Miller, MD, University of Chicago

Meredith Minkler, DrPH, University of California, Berkeley

Jim Mold, MD, University of Oklahoma

Sylvia L. Parsons, National Center for Research Resources, NIH

Valerie Robison, DDS, MPH, PhD, Centers for Disease Control
  and Prevention

Eduardo Simoes, MD, MSc, MPH, Centers for Disease Control
  and Prevention

Bernard Talbot, MD, PhD, National Center for Research Resources, NIH

Nina Wallerstein, DrPH, University of New Mexico

Anne Willoughby, MD, MPH, National Center for Research Resources, NIH

PUBLICATION DEVELOPMENT

This publication was developed as part of the work of the Clinical and Translational Science Awards (CTSA) Consortium's Community Engagement Key Function Committee. Recognizing that community involvement is essential to the identification of health concerns and interventions, the Committee created a task force on updating the 1997 publication *Principles of Community Engagement,* published by the Centers for Disease Control and Prevention and the Agency for Toxic Substances and Disease Registry. This project has been funded in whole with federal funds from the National Center for Research Resources, National Institutes of Health, through the CTSA program, part of the Roadmap Initiative, Re-Engineering the Clinical Research Enterprise. The manuscript was approved by the CTSA Consortium Publications Committee. Publication development was a collaborative effort of the CTSA Community Engagement Key Function Committee, which included members from the National Institutes of Health, Agency for Toxic Substances and Disease Registry, and Centers for Disease Control and Prevention. This publication is in the public domain and may be reprinted or copied without permission.

About the Developers

The National Institutes of Health is a part of the U.S. Department of Health and Human Services. Its mission is making important medical discoveries that improve health and save lives (www.nih.gov).

The Centers for Disease Control and Prevention is a part of the U.S. Department of Health and Human Services and is the nation's prevention agency. Its mission is to promote health and quality of life by preventing and controlling disease, injury, and disability (www.cdc.gov).

The Agency for Toxic Substances and Disease Registry is a part of the U.S. Department of Health and Human Services and is a federal public health agency. Its mission is to prevent exposure and adverse human health effects and diminished quality of life associated with exposure to hazardous substances from waste sites, unplanned releases, and other sources of pollution present in the environment (www.atsdr.cdc.gov).

For further information on the CTSA Consortium and the Community Engagement Key Function Committee, please visit www.ctsaweb.org.

The findings and conclusions in this report are those of the authors and do not necessarily represent the official position of the Centers for Disease Control and Prevention, the Agency for Toxic Substances and Disease Registry, or the National Institutes of Health.

Editorial support was provided under the American Recovery and Reinvestment Act supplemental funding to the Duke CTSA, grant number UL1RR024128, and by Palladian Partners, Inc., contract number 3035468.

Foreword

FOREWORD

As Surgeon General, I am privileged to serve as "America's Doctor," overseeing the operations of the U.S. Public Health Service and providing Americans with the best scientific information available on how to improve their health and reduce the risk of illness and injury.

In this capacity, and from my many years of family practice, I am convinced that Americans need to live and work in environments where they can practice healthy behaviors and obtain quality medical care. Social, cultural, physical, and economic foundations are important factors in the overall health of the community. We must use our resources to increase availability of healthy foods, ensure that neighborhoods have safe places for physical activity, and provide access to affordable, high-quality medical services.

Creating these healthy environments for people of all ages will require their active involvement in grassroots efforts. Private citizens, community leaders, health professionals, and researchers will need to work together to make the changes that will allow such environments to flourish.

Across the United States, coalitions are working together to create change, and we are already seeing results. The most effective collaborations include representation from various sectors—businesses, clinicians, schools, academia, government, and the faith-based community.

This work is not easy, but it is essential. When *Principles of Community Engagement* was first published in 1997, it filled an important vacuum, providing community members, health professionals, and researchers with clear principles to guide and assess their collaborative efforts. The need for such guidance has not lessened in the subsequent years. Our health challenges continue. Support for collaborative work has grown, but with this growing support has come an increasing volume and diversity of initiatives, terminology, approaches, and literature.

This new edition of *Principles* adheres to the same key principles laid out in the original booklet. It distills critical messages from the growing body of information and commentary on this topic. At the same time, it provides more detailed practical information about the application of the principles, and it responds to changes in our larger social context, including the increasing use of "virtual communities" and the growing interest in community-engaged health research.

As we continue to try to improve our nation's health, we must work together and keep in mind the community contexts that shape our health and well-being.

This is the charge and the challenge laid out in these pages.

Regina M. Benjamin, M.D., M.B.A.
Vice Admiral, U.S. Public Health Service
Surgeon General

Executive Summary

EXECUTIVE SUMMARY

Involving the community and collaborating with its members are cornerstones of efforts to improve public health. In recent years, for example, community engagement and mobilization have been essential to programs addressing smoking cessation, obesity, cancer, heart disease, and other health concerns (Ahmed et al., 2010; Minkler et al., 2008). In October 1995, recognizing the importance of involving the community, the Centers for Disease Control and Prevention (CDC) established the Committee for Community Engagement, which was composed of representatives from across CDC and the Agency for Toxic Substances and Disease Registry (ATSDR). Two years later, that committee developed the booklet *Principles of Community Engagement*, which was published by CDC and ATSDR. *Principles* defined community engagement as "the process of working collaboratively with groups of people who are affiliated by geographic proximity, special interests, or similar situations with respect to issues affecting their well-being" (CDC, 1997, p. 9). We will refer to this second edition as a primer rather than a booklet because of its expanded size and scope.

The challenges faced by the health system in 1997 are not so different from those of today, but the scope, scale, and urgency of these problems have all sharply increased. In 1997, the newly enacted Children's Health Insurance Program expanded access to health care for millions of children; today the newly enacted Patient Protection and Affordable Care Act expands access to tens of millions of people of all ages. In 1997, obesity rates had reached 20–24% in three states; today, nine states have obesity rates over 30% (CDC, 2010), and the U.S. faces unprecedented increases in the prevalence of chronic diseases, such as diabetes, hypertension, and cardiovascular disorders (CDC, 2009). Not surprisingly, community engagement is increasingly recognized as a vital component of efforts to expand access to quality care, prevent disease, and achieve health equity for all Americans.

Although the principles of community engagement laid out in 1997 have not changed, the body of knowledge supporting them has grown, and more agencies and organizations are involved in promoting community engagement and community-engaged research. CDC is now joined by the National Institutes of Health, the Health Resources and Services Administration, the U.S. Department of Veterans Affairs, and other federal agencies, academic institutions, and community partners in advancing knowledge about community engagement and in promoting its use to solve some of our more challenging problems.

Principles of Community Engagement (Second Edition) provides public health professionals, health care providers, researchers, and community-based leaders and organizations with both a science base and practical guidance for engaging partners in projects that may affect them. The principles of engagement can be used by people in a range of roles, from the program funder who needs to know how to support community engagement to the researcher or community leader who needs hands-on, practical information on how to mobilize the members of a community to partner in research initiatives. In addition, this primer provides tools for those who are leading efforts to improve population health through community engagement.

In the context of engagement, "community" has been understood in two ways. It is sometimes used to refer to those who are affected by the health issues being addressed. This use recognizes that the community as defined in this way has historically been left out of health improvement efforts even though it is supposed to be the beneficiary of those efforts. On the other hand, "community" can be used in a more general way, illustrated by referring to stakeholders such as academics, public health professionals, and policy makers as communities. This use has the advantage of recognizing that every group has its own particular culture and norms and that anyone can take the lead in engagement efforts. In this second edition of *Principles of Community Engagement,* we recognize the need for particular attention to engagement of communities affected by health issues. We also promote the idea that engagement for health improvement can be initiated and led by the "lay" community rather than professional groups. Regardless, we recognize that the groups involved in community engagement have their own particular norms and that all partners in a collaboration will have lessons to learn about each other and the collaborative process. Moreover, we fully appreciate that all who are involved in engaging a community must be responsive to the needs of that community as defined by the community itself.

In practice, community engagement is a blend of science and art. The science comes from sociology, political science, cultural anthropology, organizational development, psychology, social work, and other disciplines, and organizing concepts are drawn from the literature on community participation, community mobilization, constituency building, community psychology, and cultural influences. The art comes from the understanding, skill, and sensitivity used to apply and adapt the science in ways that fit the community of interest and the purposes of specific engagement efforts. The results of these efforts may be defined differently and can encompass a broad range of structures (e.g., coalitions, partnerships, collaborations), but they all fall under the general rubric of community engagement and are treated similarly in this primer.

This primer can serve as a guide for understanding the principles of community engagement for those who are developing or implementing a community engagement plan, or it can be a resource for students or faculty. Community processes can be complex and labor-intensive, and they require dedicated resources such as time, funding, and people with the necessary skills. Leaders everywhere are struggling with how to make the right choices as they try to improve health care services and promote individual and population health. Readers of this primer may find that a fuller understanding of community engagement will facilitate and promote its use and thus advance the health of all of our communities.

ORGANIZATION OF THE *PRINCIPLES OF COMMUNITY ENGAGEMENT*

The first of this primer's eight chapters reviews organizing concepts, models, and frameworks from the literature, and the second chapter introduces the principles of community engagement, which are rooted in that literature. As in the first edition, one chapter contains a series of community case examples (Chapter 3) taken from the literature on community engagement that link to the principles described in Chapter 2. Chapter 4 describes how to manage organizational support for community engagement; this chapter reflects our growing awareness of the challenges of putting community engagement into practice. Chapter 5 addresses the increased interest in community-engaged research, and Chapter 6 deals with the rapidly changing world of social networking. Chapter 7 deals with evaluation, and Chapter 8 offers a brief summary and closing remarks.

This primer was written as an integrated whole, with later chapters building on those that come before. Even so, the chapters can also stand alone and be used as needed. This is by intention, as we wish to meet the needs of our diverse audiences. We hope that whoever uses *Principles* (Second Edition) finds it helpful in assisting their efforts to engage communities.

REFERENCES

Ahmed SM, Palermo AG. Community engagement in research: frameworks for education and peer review. *American Journal of Public Health* 2010;100(8):1380-1387.

Centers for Disease Control and Prevention. *Chronic diseases. The power to prevent, the call to control: at a glance 2009.* Atlanta (GA): Centers for Disease Control and Prevention; 2009. Retrieved from http://www.cdc.gov/chronicdisease/resources/publications/AAG/pdf/chronic.pdf.

Centers for Disease Control and Prevention. *Obesity trends among U.S. adults between 1985 and 2009.* Atlanta (GA): Centers for Disease Control and Prevention; 2010. Retrieved from http://www.cdc.gov/obesity/downloads/obesity_trends_2009.pdf.

Centers for Disease Control and Prevention. *Principles of community engagement* (1st ed.). Atlanta (GA): CDC/ATSDR Committee on Community Engagement; 1997.

Minkler M, Wallerstein N. The growing support for CBPR. In: Minkler M, Wallerstein N (editors). *Community-based participatory research for health: from process to outcomes* (2nd ed., p. 544). San Francisco: Jossey-Bass; 2008.

Community Engagement:

Definitions and Organizing Concepts from the Literature

Chapter 1
Community Engagement:
Definitions and Organizing Concepts from the Literature

Donna Jo McCloskey, RN, PhD, (Chair), Mary Anne McDonald, DrPH, MA, Jennifer Cook, MPH, Suzanne Heurtin-Roberts, PhD, MSW, Stephen Updegrove, MD, MPH, Dana Sampson, MS, MBA, Sheila Gutter, PhD, Milton (Mickey) Eder, PhD

INTRODUCTION

Over the last two decades, research and practice in health promotion have increasingly employed community engagement, defined as "the process of working collaboratively with and through groups of people affiliated by geographic proximity, special interest, or similar situations to address issues affecting the well-being of those people" (Centers for Disease Control and Prevention [CDC], 1997, p. 9). In general, the goals of community engagement are to build trust, enlist new resources and allies, create better communication, and improve overall health outcomes as successful projects evolve into lasting collaborations (CDC, 1997; Shore, 2006; Wallerstein, 2002).

The rationale for community-engaged health promotion, policy making, and research is largely rooted in the recognition that lifestyles, behaviors, and the incidence of illness are all shaped by social and physical environments (Hanson, 1988; Institute of Medicine, 1988). This "ecological" view is consistent with the idea that health inequalities have their roots in larger socioeconomic conditions (Iton, 2009). If health is socially determined, then health issues are best addressed by engaging community partners who can bring their own perspectives and understandings of community life and health issues to a project. And if health inequalities are rooted in larger socioeconomic inequalities, then approaches to health improvement must take into account the concerns of communities and be able to benefit diverse populations.

The growing commitment to community engagement is reflected in a number of major federal initiatives, including the Clinical and Translational Science Awards (CTSA) program and the Research Centers in Minority Institutions program of the National Institutes of Health (NIH), CDC's Prevention Research Centers, and the practice-based research networks of the Agency for Healthcare Research and Quality (AHRQ). In addition, new work by AHRQ highlights the potential benefits of engaging patients and families in the redesign of medical care (Scholle et al., 2010). Healthy People 2020, which lays out our national health objectives, emphasizes collaboration among diverse groups as a strategy to improve health.

This emphasis on community engagement has encouraged health professionals, community leaders, and policy makers to imagine new opportunities as they face new challenges (Doll et al., 2008). This initial chapter addresses concepts, models, and frameworks that can be used to guide and inspire efforts to meet those challenges. It does not pretend to cover all the available and relevant social science and public health literature, but it provides an overview of some of the critical organizing concepts that shed light on the idea of community and the practice of community engagement. Sociology, political science, cultural anthropology, organizational development, psychology, social work, and other disciplines have all contributed to the development and practice of community engagement (Minkler et al., 2009). Moreover, community engagement is grounded in the principles of community organization: fairness, justice, empowerment, participation, and self-determination (Alinsky, 1962; Chávez et al., 2007; Freire, 1970; Wallerstein et al., 2006). The interdisciplinary background offered in this chapter provides a rich array of concepts for stakeholders, such as public health agencies, practice-based researchers (in

> Moreover, community engagement is grounded in the principles of community organization: fairness, justice, empowerment, participation, and self-determination...

clinics, agencies, after-school programs, and nursing homes), policy makers, and community organizations, to draw from when developing partnerships in community engagement.

This chapter is more extensive than the corresponding chapter in the first edition, reflecting growth in the literature and the increased collective experience in community engagement.

CONCEPTS OF COMMUNITY

There are many ways to think about community. We will explore four of the most relevant, each of which provides different insights into the process of community engagement.

Systems Perspective

From a systems perspective, a community is similar to a living creature, comprising different parts that represent specialized functions, activities, or interests, each operating within specific boundaries to meet community needs. For example, schools focus on education, the transportation sector focuses on moving people and products, economic entities focus on enterprise and employment, faith organizations focus on the spiritual and physical well-being of people, and health care agencies focus on the prevention and treatment of diseases and injuries (Henry, 2011). For the community to function well, each part has to effectively carry out its role *in relation to the whole organism.* A healthy community has well-connected, interdependent sectors that share responsibility for recognizing and resolving problems and enhancing its well-being. Successfully addressing a community's complex problems requires integration, collaboration, and coordination of resources from all parts (Thompson et al., 1990). From a systems perspective, then, collaboration is a logical approach to health improvement.

Social Perspective

A community can also be defined by describing the social and political networks that link individuals, community organizations, and leaders. Understanding these networks is critical to planning efforts in engagement. For example, tracing social ties among individuals may help engagement leaders to identify a community's leadership, understand its behavior patterns, identify its high-risk groups, and strengthen its networks (Minkler et al., 1997). Chapter 6 explores this approach to understanding a community in greater depth.

Virtual Perspective

Some communities map onto geographically defined areas, but today, individuals rely more and more on computer-mediated communications to access information, meet people, and make decisions that affect their lives (Kozinets, 2002). Examples of computer-mediated forms of communication include email, instant or text messaging, e-chat rooms, and social networking sites such as Facebook, YouTube, and Twitter (Flavian et al., 2005). Social groups or groups with a common interest that interact in an organized fashion on the Internet are considered "virtual communities" (Rheingold, 2000; Ridings et al., 2002). Without question, these virtual communities are potential partners for community-engaged health promotion and research. Chapter 6 focuses on social networking and expands on the virtual perspective.

Individual Perspective

Individuals have their own sense of community membership that is beyond the definitions of community applied by researchers and engagement leaders. Moreover, they may have a sense of belonging to more than one community. In addition, their sense of membership can change over time and may affect their participation in community activities (Minkler et al., 2004).

The philosopher and psychologist William James shed light on this issue in his writings. James thought it important to consider two perspectives on identity: the "I," or how a person thinks about himself or herself, and the "me," or how others see and think about that person. Sometimes these two views agree and result in a shared sense of an identity, but other times they do not. People should not make assumptions about identity based on appearance, language, or cultural origin; nor should they make assumptions about an individual's perspective based on his or her identity (James, 1890). Today, the multiple communities that might be relevant for any individual — including families, workplace, and social, religious, and political associations — suggest that individuals are thinking about themselves in more complex ways than was the norm in years past.

The eligibility criteria that scientists, policy makers, and others develop for social programs and research projects reflect one way that people perceive a group of proposed participants, but how much those criteria reflect the participants' actual view of themselves is uncertain. Practitioners of community engagement need to learn how individuals understand their identity and connections, enter into relationships, and form communities.

WHAT IS COMMUNITY ENGAGEMENT?

In the first edition of *Principles,* the authors developed a working definition of community engagement that captures its key features:

> ...the process of working collaboratively with and through groups of people affiliated by geographic proximity, special interest, or similar situations to address issues affecting the well-being of those people. It is a powerful vehicle for bringing about environmental and behavioral changes that will improve the health of the community and its members. It often involves partnerships and coalitions that help mobilize resources and influence systems, change relationships among partners, and serve as catalysts for changing policies, programs, and practices (CDC, 1997, p. 9).

Community engagement can take many forms, and partners can include organized groups, agencies, institutions, or individuals. Collaborators may be engaged in health promotion, research, or policy making.

Community engagement can also be seen as a continuum of community involvement. Figure 1.1 below, modified from a diagram originally drawn by the International Association for Public Participation, illustrates one way of thinking about such a continuum. Over time, a specific collaboration is likely to move along this continuum toward greater community involvement, and any given collaboration is likely to evolve in other ways, too. Most notably, while community engagement may be achieved during a time-limited project, it frequently involves — and often evolves into — long-term partnerships that move from the traditional focus on a single health issue to address a range of social, economic, political, and environmental factors that affect health.

Community engagement can take many forms, and partners can include organized groups, agencies, institutions, or individuals. Collaborators may be engaged in health promotion, research, or policy making.

| Increasing Level of Community Involvement, Impact, Trust, and Communication Flow ➤ |

Outreach	Consult	Involve	Collaborate	Shared Leadership
Some Community Involvement *Communication flows from one to the other, to inform* Provides community with information. Entities coexist. Outcomes: Optimally, establishes communication channels and channels for outreach.	*More Community Involvement* *Communication flows to the community and then back, answer seeking* Gets information or feedback from the community. Entities share information. Outcomes: Develops connections.	*Better Community Involvement* *Communication flows both ways, participatory form of communication* Involves more participation with community on issues. Entities cooperate with each other. Outcomes: Visibility of partnership established with increased cooperation.	Community Involvement *Communication flow is bidirectional* Forms partnerships with community on each aspect of project from development to solution. Entities form bidirectional communication channels. Outcomes: Partnership building, trust building.	*Strong Bidirectional Relationship* Final decision making is at community level. Entities have formed strong partnership structures. Outcomes: Broader health outcomes affecting broader community. Strong bidirectional trust built.

Reference: Modified by the authors from the International Association for Public Participation.

Figure 1.1. Community Engagement Continuum

Why Practice Community Engagement?

Advocates of community engagement assert that it improves health promotion and health research. However, the processes, costs, and benefits of community engagement are still a relatively new field of study. In 2004, AHRQ brought attention to the importance of empirical work in this area and greatly advanced our knowledge through a synthesis of the research, much of which indicated that community engagement strengthened the conduct of research (Viswanathan et al., 2004).

A recent review of the literature on community engagement identified nine areas in which community engagement made a positive impact (Staley, 2009). Although this study focused on research partnerships, many of its findings are relevant to community engagement in general. The nine areas and the corresponding benefits were as follows:

1. **Agenda**—Engagement changes the choice and focus of projects, how they are initiated, and their potential to obtain funding. New areas for collaboration are identified, and funding that requires community engagement becomes accessible.

2. **Design and delivery**—Improvements to study design, tools, interventions, representation/participation, data collection and analysis, communication, and dissemination can be implemented. New interventions or previously unappreciated causal links can be identified through the community's knowledge of local circumstances. The speed and efficiency of the project can be enhanced by rapidly engaging partners and participants and identifying new sources of information.

3. **Implementation and change**—Improvements can be made in the way research findings are used to bring about change (e.g., through new or improved services, policy or funding changes, or transformation of professional practices), and capacity for change and the maintenance of long-term partnerships can be expanded.

4. **Ethics**—Engagement creates opportunities to improve the consent process, identify ethical pitfalls, and create processes for resolving ethical problems when they arise.

5. **The public involved in the project**—The knowledge and skills of the public involved in the project can be enhanced, and their contributions can be recognized (possibly through financial rewards). These efforts foster goodwill and help lay the groundwork for subsequent collaborations.

6. **Academic partners**—Academic partners can gain enhanced understanding of the issue under study and appreciation of the role and value of community involvement, which sometimes result in direct career benefits. In addition, new insights into the relevance of a project and the various benefits to be gained from it can result in increased opportunities to disseminate its findings and their wider use.

7. **Individual research participants**—Improvements in the way studies are carried out can make it easier to participate in them and bring benefits to participants.

8. **Community organizations**—These organizations can gain enhanced knowledge, a higher profile in the community, more linkages with other community members and entities, and new organizational capacity. These benefits can create goodwill and help lay the groundwork for subsequent collaborations.

9. **The general public**—The general public is likely to be more receptive to the research and reap greater benefits from it.

The author of the review acknowledged that there can be costs associated with community engagement (e.g., increased time and other resource needs, the need to develop new skill sets, increased expectations) but contended that these are more than outweighed by the positive impacts and generally can be addressed over time through training and experience (Staley, 2009).

USEFUL CONCEPTS FOR THE PRACTICE OF COMMUNITY ENGAGEMENT

The social science and public health fields provide us not only with useful definitions of community and ideas about community engagement but also with a wealth of concepts that are relevant to the practice of engagement. Here, we explore some of the most important.

Culture and Community Engagement

One of the more useful of the hundreds of definitions of culture is this one from the anthropologist Christie Kiefer (2007): "a complex integrated system of thought and behavior shared by members of a group — a system whose whole pattern allows us to understand the meanings that people attach to specific facts and observations." Culture shapes identities and fosters notions of community, and it shapes how individuals and groups relate to each other, how meaning is created, and how power is defined. Furthermore, culture shapes ideas about partnership, trust, and negotiation. Therefore, culture shapes the process of community engagement, and effective engagement requires an understanding of culture (Blumenthal et al., 2004; Dévieux et al., 2005; Silka et al., 2008).

In particular, researchers and practitioners need to understand the cultural dynamics of specific groups and institutions in order to build relationships, identify ways to effectively collaborate, and build respect and trust. This is an ongoing effort for all involved in the community engagement process (Harrell et al., 2006; Minkler et al., 2004; Shoultz et al., 2006; Sullivan et al., 2001). Communities are not homogeneous entities; they are made up of diverse groups with different histories, social structures, value systems, and cultural understandings of the world.

There is no question that culture and health are intimately connected. Indeed, culture influences perceptions of illness and suffering, methods of disease prevention, treatments for illness, and use of health services. Both medical and public health literature recognize the connection between health and culture (Airhihenbuwa, 2007; Fisher et al., 2007; Krumeich et al., 2001; Resnicow et al., 1999), but the solution to bridging cultural boundaries is often presented as acquiring "cultural competency," or having knowledge of a group's cultural differences and typical behaviors or beliefs. This is inadequate, however. As anthropologists have demonstrated, culture is dynamic and complex, and cultural competence is more than identifying how a group is thought to differ from prevailing standards or norms of behavior and belief (Carpenter-Song et al., 2007). Focusing on the meanings that individuals share and on the explanatory models they use to discuss their health problems provides a richer understanding of these individuals and can yield a cultural understanding that is rooted in their real lives rather than in stereotypes. This meaning-centered approach can also help reveal how community conditions are determined by social, economic, and political forces rather than simply by individual choices (Carpenter-Song et al., 2007; Kleinman et al., 2006; Kumagai et al., 2009; Silka et al., 2008).

To achieve successful collaboration with a community, all parties involved need to strive to understand the point of view of "insiders," whether they are members of a neighborhood, religious institution, health practice, community organization, or public health agency. Key to developing such understanding is recognizing one's *own* culture and how it shapes one's beliefs and understanding of health and illness (Airhihenbuwa, 2007; Hahn, 1999; Harrell et al., 2006; Kleinman, 1980; Minkler, 2004). For example, community-engaged programs and research often involve people from universities or health institutions working with community groups in areas labeled "low income" or "at risk." Acknowledging diversity in background, experience, culture, income, and education and examining how society produces privilege, racism, and inequalities in power should be central to the process of community engagement. Such an approach can help partners better understand and address the roots of health issues and guard against reproducing repressive patterns within their partnerships (Chávez et al., 2008; Chavez et al., 2007; Jones et al., 2000; Krieger et al., 1999; Yonas et al., 2006).

To achieve successful collaboration with a community, all parties involved need to strive to understand the point of view of "insiders," whether they are members of a neighborhood, religious institution, health practice, community organization, or public health agency.

Done well, the community-engaged approach can enable partnerships to develop programs and research "in ways that are consistent with a people's and a community's cultural framework" (Airhihenbuwa, 1995). When researchers and organizers work collaboratively with community organizations throughout a project, they can produce effective, culturally appropriate programs and robust research results.

Community Organization

The practice and theory of community organizing provide useful insights into mobilizing the community to engage in health promotion. The foundation for community organizing is the principle of social action, bringing people together — often, but not exclusively, from the same neighborhood — to pursue a shared interest (Braithwaite et al., 1994).

When pursuing social action, a key question is who represents the community. Often, the most empowered members of a community will quickly move to the forefront, regardless of whether they are truly the most representative (Geiger, 1984). Similarly, engagement leaders may want to work with those who can most readily deliver what they want (such as research participants and data sources), but these persons may not be representative of the community. Facilitating community organization cannot be allowed to serve the needs of individual partners at the expense of the larger community (CARE: Community Alliance for Research and Engagement, 2009).

Community organizing is based on the principles of empowerment, community competence, active participation, and "starting where the people are" (Nyswander, 1956, as cited in Minkler, 2005, p. 27). As Labonte et al. (1996) state, imposing one's own notions of health concerns over the community's risks several disabling effects. These include being irrelevant to the community, creating feelings of powerlessness in the community, complicating individuals' lives, and channeling local activism away from important challenges toward less important ones.

Community organizing recognizes that, in order to change, we all must feel a need for change, and that we are more likely to do so when we are involved in group learning and decision making (Minkler, 1990). An important element of community organizing is helping communities look at the root causes of problems while at the same time selecting issues that are "winnable, simple, and specific" and that can unite members of the group, involve them in achieving a solution, and further build the community (Minkler, 1990).

Community Participation

Community engagement requires participation of community members in projects that address their issues. Meaningful community participation extends beyond physical involvement to include generation of ideas, contributions to decision making, and sharing of responsibility. Among the factors that motivate people to participate are wanting to play an active role in bettering their own lives, fulfilling social or religious obligations, feeling a need for a sense of community, and wanting cash or in-kind rewards. Whatever people's motivations, obtaining meaningful community participation and having a successful, sustained initiative require that engagement leaders respect, listen to, and learn from community members. An absence of mutual respect and co-learning can result in a loss of time, trust, resources, and, most importantly, effectiveness (Henry, 2011; Miller et al., 2005; Minkler et al., 2009).

> Meaningful community participation extends beyond physical involvement to include generation of ideas, contributions to decision making, and sharing of responsibility.

The "social exchange" perspective provides insight into motivations for participation; it uses the framework of benefits and costs to help explain who participates and why. From this perspective, organizations and individuals are involved in an "exchange system" and voluntarily share resources to meet their goals (Levine et al., 1961). Community members and organizations will participate if they perceive that the benefits of participation outweigh the effort required (Butterfoss, 2006; Butterfoss et al., 1993; Wandersman et al., 1987).

The potential benefits of participation for community members, academics, and health professionals include opportunities for networking, access to information and resources, personal recognition, learning, a sense of helping to solve community problems, improved relationships among stakeholders, increased capacity for problem solving, and contact with hard-to-reach populations (Butterfoss, 2006). Costs include the time and energy required to build relationships and other infrastructure and the lessening of control over initiatives (Staley, 2009).

Recently, literature has shifted from a focus on a social exchange model to other challenges and facilitators of community participation (Shalowitz et al., 2009). Some of these writings are based on experience rather than theory, but they may lead to the development of improved theories of participation (Michener et al., 2008; Williams et al., 2009).

Robert Putnam (2001) initiated an important debate about the degree to which Americans volunteer for and participate in group and community activities with the publication of *Bowling Alone*. In the book, Putnam argued that the willingness to volunteer and participate in public life waxes and wanes over time but that overall it has declined in recent decades. If there is indeed a trend away from civic engagement, it would affect efforts to engage communities in improving health.

Regardless of whether one agrees with Putnam's assessment, it is essential to recognize that the community's time is valuable and limited. Furthermore, developing relationships with individuals and community organizations, identifying common interests, and developing a shared sense of needs and shared ways to address those needs can take engagement leaders and stakeholders an enormous amount of time. Given the expanded roles that community members are being asked to play in the development of social programs and in research, we must consider how to compensate them for their participation, and we should involve them in this process.

The costs, benefits, and perceived risks of participation can sometimes be changed with collaborative planning and decision making. For example, academic partners have traditionally presumed ownership of any data or other tangibles resulting from research, but if the benefits of participation are to outweigh the costs and the principles of community engagement are to be met, the community should be involved early on in identifying what assets the research will produce and the rights of each partner to use those assets (see Yale Center for Clinical Investigation/Community Alliance for Research and Engagement, 2009).

Constituency Development

Developing a constituency, or developing relationships with community members who have a stake in and support public health and health care, involves four "practice elements":

- Know the community, its constituents, and its capabilities.

- Establish positions and strategies that guide interactions with constituents.

- Build and sustain formal and informal networks to maintain relationships, communicate messages, and leverage resources.

- Mobilize communities and constituencies for decision making and social action (Hatcher et al., 2008).

These four elements, which provide a simple, useful framework for thinking about the requirements of community engagement, will be revisited in Chapter 4's discussion of the organizational support required for community engagement.

Capacity Building

Building capacity to improve health involves the development of sustainable skills, resources, and organizational structures in the affected community. For engagement efforts to be equitable, effective, and sustainable, all stakeholders must be ready for collaboration and leadership. Thus, building capacity also includes fostering shared knowledge, leadership skills, and an ability to represent the interests of one's constituents. Because capacity building is deeply rooted in the social, political, and economic environment, it cannot be conducted without an understanding of the specific environment in which it will take place (Eng et al., 1994). When carried out with context in mind, capacity building is an integral part of community engagement efforts, necessary for challenging power imbalances and effectively addressing problems.

> Building capacity to improve health involves the development of sustainable skills, resources, and organizational structures in the affected community.

Community Empowerment

The theoretical roots of "empowerment" as a critical element of community engagement can be traced back to Brazilian educator Paolo Freire (Freire, 1970; Hur, 2006). As articulated by Kenneth Maton (2008), empowerment is "a group-based participatory, developmental process through which marginalized or oppressed individuals and groups gain greater control over their lives and environment, acquire valued resources and basic rights, and achieve important life goals and reduced societal marginalization." Ideally, empowerment is both a process and an outcome of community engagement.

> Empowerment takes place at three levels: the individual, the organization or group, and the community.

Empowerment takes place at three levels: the individual, the organization or group, and the community. Empowerment at one level can influence empowerment at the other levels. Furthermore, empowerment is multidimensional, taking place in sociological, psychological, economic, political, and other dimensions (Fawcett et al., 1995; Hur, 2006; Maton, 2008; Rich et al., 1995). Community-level empowerment "challenges professional relationships to communities, emphasizing partnership and collaboration rather than a top-down approach" (Wallerstein, 2002, p. 74).

Empowerment theory stresses that no external entity should assume that it can bestow on a community the power to act in its own self-interest. Rather, those working to engage the community should, when appropriate, offer tools and resources to help the community act in its own interest. This could include helping to channel existing sources of community power in new ways to act on the determinants of health. Kretzmann et al. (1996) note that communities are usually assessed in terms of their problems, but they point out that this demeans and disempowers the community, relegating its members to the roles of dependents and recipients of services. They advocate for assessing communities in terms of their own assets, resources, and resourcefulness (Kretzmann et al., 1996).

Coalition Building

Community engagement often involves building coalitions, defined by Cohen et al. (2002) as "a union of people and organizations working to influence outcomes on a specific problem" (p. 144). The goals of a coalition might range from sharing information and resources to advocating for specific policy changes (Cohen et al., 2002). Increasingly, funders have supported the building of coalitions for improving community health (Butterfoss et al., 1993; Green et al., 2001a; Hill et al., 2007).

The motivation to create coalitions comes from the recognition that they can accomplish what each partner cannot accomplish alone. Political science literature suggests that:

- Coalitions require that each party believe it needs help to reach its goals.

- The goals and perspectives of the members of a coalition will not all be shared. However, the coalition requires sufficient common ground that the parties can agree over time on a purpose, set of policies, and strategies.

- Coalitions require continuous and often delicate negotiation among their participants.

- The distribution of power and benefits among the members of a coalition is an ongoing concern; all members need to believe that, over time, they are receiving benefits that are comparable to their contributions (Sofaer, 1993).

Coalitions can help the engagement process in a number of ways, including maximizing the influence of individuals and organizations, creating new collective resources, and reducing the duplication of efforts. The effectiveness of coalitions has been evaluated on two distinct bases: how well the members work together, and what kinds of community-level changes they bring about. While noting that the research literature is inadequate for determining which factors are associated with the effectiveness of coalitions, Zakocs et al. (2006) suggest six possibilities: formalization of rules/procedures, leadership style, participation of members, diversity of membership, collaboration, and group cohesion.

Based on their review of the literature on coalitions, Butterfoss et al. (2002) developed community coalition action theory, which provides 23 practice-based propositions that address processes ranging from the formation of coalitions through the institutionalization of long-lasting coalitions. These propositions, which shed light on how to create and support effective long-term alliances, will be discussed in greater detail in Chapter 4.

THE ETHICS OF COMMUNITY ENGAGED RESEARCH

Debates about the ethics of clinical research are not new (Chen et al., 2006; Emanuel et al., 2000; Levine, 1988), but community-engaged research (CEnR)

Community engagement is about relationships between and among communities, researchers, and research institutions.

raises additional questions and challenges. Community engagement is about relationships between and among communities, researchers, and research institutions. What ethical code should we use to assess the conduct of those relationships, and how should that code be monitored and enforced? As CEnR has become more prevalent and more varied, this fundamental question has generated a number of specific questions and ideas (Khanlou et al., 2005; Silverstein et al., 2008).

A well-accepted ethical code concerning research that involves living human beings already exists, and a regulatory process based in this code has been developed for all federally funded "human subjects research." The need for this ethical code stems from the nature of research — by definition, that which is being researched has not yet been "proven." Accordingly, there is uncertainty about the results of research activities, including the possibility of harm to participants. In this ethical framework, studies are understood to fall into two general categories: those that present minimal risk to participants, and those that may subject participants to more than minimal risk (see Common Rule 45 CFR [Code of Federal Regulations] 46.102(h)(i)).

All federally funded research that involves living people requires review by an institutional review board (IRB); the people who serve on IRBs and review research have a responsibility to ensure that risk to participants is minimized. The issues that IRBs consider include the risks to participants, the procedures for collecting and protecting research data, the strength of the scientific design, and the process by which individuals give their informed consent to participate in research.

Should there be a process for determining whether a CEnR collaboration is based on trust and whether each partner has successfully fulfilled his or her responsibilities to the other partners and to the project? If there should be such a process or similar processes, should they be the responsibility of the IRB? In their reviews, IRBs typically have not considered many activities and principles of community engagement. For example, although IRBs may require letters of support from community partners, they are not concerned with how well the researcher knows the community or whether trust has been established. Once research has been approved, the IRB will not typically obtain community input for its regular reviews of research protocols. Furthermore, studies demonstrate that IRBs generally do not incorporate the principles of CEnR into their considerations, even for studies that are community engaged (Flicker et al. 2007), and some have questioned whether the current IRB system is appropriate to provide oversight for all forms of CEnR (Brugge et al., 2003; Malone et al., 2006; Ross et al., 2010a, 2010b, 2010c; Shore, 2007). Finally, the majority of IRBs do not want to take on this additional task, and researchers and others are wary of "IRB mission creep" as these boards take on more and more regulatory responsibility (Center for Advanced Study, 2004).

The Yale University CTSA's Community Alliance for Research and Engagement (CARE) Ethical Principles of Engagement Committee (2009) developed an expanded set of principles that is relevant to this discussion. The committee's view is that ethical review applies "not only to individual research subjects but also to interactions between the research partners" (p. 2). The committee explains: "Each partner has certain responsibilities. Among the most important of these is that each should recognize the other's needs and empower the other to assert its unique rights within the relationship" (CARE, 2009, p. 9).

Part of ethical conduct is developing a legitimate and serious dissemination plan for the findings of the proposed research that will meet the needs of both communities and researchers. In addition to its emphasis on ethical and empowering practice among partnership organizations, the CARE Committee extends the principles and protections of the Belmont Report to communities:

> University Researchers should involve Community partners as early as possible in discussions about the potential uses of all data to be collected, including a dissemination plan for the sharing of the research findings with the wider [non-academic] Community, and should develop a process for handling findings that may reflect negatively and thus cause harm to one or both partners (CARE, 2009, p. 3).

Others have called for ethical review to consider the risks and benefits for both individual participants and entire communities and are asking whether it should be required that communities, as well as individuals, consent to research. This issue is particularly relevant for research into the relationship between the environment and health because the discovery and dissemination of environmental information may affect the well-being of an entire community (Brown et al., 2006; Gbadegesin et al., 2006; Shore,

2006; Wing, 2002). There is also uncertainty about the roles and authority of community advisory boards and what ethical principles, if any, govern these boards (Blumenthal, 2006; Gilbert, 2006; Quinn, 2004).

Developing a comprehensive list of ethical questions for CEnR is challenging because the purpose, approach, and context for such research varies greatly from one project to another (Green et al., 2001b; Israel et al., 1988). As both the volume and range of CEnR activities that focus on health expand, ideas about the ethical review of such research, both inside and outside the health field, will continue to develop.

MODELS AND FRAMEWORKS FOR THE PRACTICE OF COMMUNITY ENGAGEMENT

In addition to the concepts just summarized, the literature provides models and frameworks for understanding health promotion and health research that can be helpful in the practice of community engagement. We cover a number of those here.

The Social Ecological Model of Health

The social ecological model conceptualizes health broadly and focuses on multiple factors that might affect health. This broad approach to thinking of health, advanced in the 1947 Constitution of the World Health Organization, includes physical, mental, and social well-being (World Health Organization, 1947). The social ecological model understands health to be affected by the interaction between the individual, the group/community, and the physical, social, and political environments (Israel et al., 2003; Sallis et al., 2008; Wallerstein et al., 2003).

> The social ecological model understands health to be affected by the interaction between the individual, the group/community, and the physical, social, and political environments.

Both the community engagement approach and the social ecological model recognize the complex role played by context in the development of health problems as well as in the success or failure of attempts to address these problems. Health professionals, researchers, and community leaders can use this model to identify factors at different levels (the individual, the interpersonal level, the community, society; see Figure 1.2) that contribute to poor health and to develop approaches to disease prevention and health promotion that include action at those levels. This approach focuses on integrating approaches to change the physical and social environments rather than modifying only individual health behaviors.

Stokols (1996) proposes four core principles that underlie the ways the social ecological model can contribute to efforts to engage communities:

- Health status, emotional well-being, and social cohesion are influenced by the physical, social, and cultural dimensions of the individual's or community's environment and personal attributes (e.g., behavior patterns, psychology, genetics).

- The same environment may have different effects on an individual's health depending on a variety of factors, including perceptions of ability to control the environment and financial resources.

- Individuals and groups operate in multiple environments (e.g., workplace, neighborhood, larger geographic communities) that "spill over" and influence each other.

- There are personal and environmental "leverage points," such as the physical environment, available resources, and social norms, that exert vital influences on health and well-being.

To inform its health promotion programs, CDC (2007) created a four-level model of the factors affecting health that is grounded in social ecological theory, as illustrated in Figure 1.2.

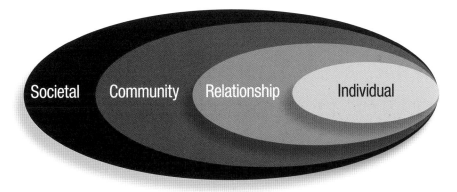

Figure 1.2. The Social-Ecological Model: A Framework for Prevention

The first level of the model (at the extreme right) includes individual biology and other personal characteristics, such as age, education, income, and health history. The second level, relationship, includes a person's closest social circle, such as friends, partners, and family members, all of whom influence a person's behavior and contribute to his or her experiences. The third level, community, explores the settings in which people have social relationships, such as schools, workplaces, and neighborhoods, and seeks to identify the characteristics of these settings that affect health. Finally, the fourth level looks at the broad societal factors that favor or impair health. Examples here include cultural and social norms and the health, economic, educational, and social policies that help to create, maintain, or lessen socioeconomic inequalities between groups (CDC, 2007; Krug et al., 2002).

The CDC model enables community-engaged partnerships to identify a comprehensive list of factors that contribute to poor health and develop a broad approach to health problems that involves actions at many levels to produce and reinforce change. For example, an effort to reduce childhood obesity might include the following activities at the four levels of interest:

- **Individual:** Conduct education programs to help people make wise choices to improve nutritional intake, increase their physical activity, and control their weight.

- **Interpersonal relationships:** Create walking clubs and work with community groups to introduce healthy menus and cooking methods. Promote community gardening groups.

- **Community:** Work with local grocery stores and convenience stores to help them increase the amount of fresh fruits and vegetables they carry. Establish farmers' markets that accept food stamps so that low-income residents can shop there. Work with the city or county to identify walking trails, parks, and indoor sites where people can go to walk, and publicize these sites. If the area needs additional venues for exercise, build community demand and lobby for new areas to be built or designated. Work with local employers to develop healthier food choices on site and to create other workplace health programs.

- **Society:** Advocate for the passage of regulations to (1) eliminate soft drinks and high-calorie snacks from all schools, (2) ban the use of trans–fatty acids in restaurant food, or (3) mandate that a percentage of the budget for road maintenance and construction be spent on creating walking paths and bike lanes.

Long-term attention to all levels of the social ecological model creates the changes and synergy needed to support sustainable improvements in health.

The Active Community Engagement Continuum

The Active Community Engagement (ACE) continuum provides a framework for analyzing community engagement and the role the community plays in influencing lasting behavior change. ACE was developed by the Access, Quality and Use in Reproductive Health (ACQUIRE) project team, which is supported by the U.S. Agency for International Development and managed by EngenderHealth in partnership with the Adventist Development and Relief Agency International, CARE, IntraHealth International, Inc., Meridian Group International, Inc., and the Society for Women and AIDS in Africa (Russell et al., 2008). The ACE continuum is based on a review of documents, best practices, and lessons learned during the ACQUIRE project; in a paper by Russell et al. (2008) the continuum is described as follows:

> The continuum consists of three levels of engagement across five characteristics of engagement. The levels of engagement, which move from consultative to cooperative to collaborative, reflect the realities of program partnerships and programs. These three levels of community engagement can be adapted, with specific activities based on these categories of action. The five characteristics of engagement are community involvement in assessment; access to information; inclusion in decision making; local capacity to advocate to institutions and governing structures; and accountability of institutions to the public (p. 6).

The experience of the ACQUIRE team shows that community engagement is not a one-time event but rather an evolutionary process. At each successive level of engagement, community members move closer to being change agents themselves rather than targets for change, and collaboration increases, as does community empowerment. At the final (collaborative) level, communities and stakeholders are represented equally in the partnership, and all parties are mutually accountable for all aspects of the project (Russell et al., 2008).

Diffusion of Innovation

Everett Rogers (1995) defined diffusion as "the process by which an innovation is communicated through certain channels over time among the members of a social system" (p. 5). Communication, in turn, according to Rogers, is a "process in which participants create and share information with one another in order to reach a mutual understanding" (p. 5). In the case of diffusion of innovation, the communication is about an idea or new approach. Understanding the diffusion process is essential to community-engaged efforts to spread innovative practices in health improvement.

Rogers offered an early formulation of the idea that there are different stages in the innovation process and that individuals move through these stages at different rates and with different concerns. Thus, diffusion of innovation provides a platform for understanding variations in how communities (or groups or individuals within communities) respond to community engagement efforts.

In Rogers' first stage, *knowledge,* the individual or group is exposed to an innovation but lacks information about it. In the second stage, *persuasion,* the individual or group is interested in the innovation and actively seeks out information. In *decision,* the third stage, the individual or group weighs the advantages and disadvantages of using the innovation and decides whether to adopt or reject it. If adoption occurs, the individual or group moves to the fourth stage, *implementation,* and employs the innovation to some degree. During this stage, the usefulness of the innovation is determined, and additional information may be sought. In the fifth stage, *confirmation,* the individual or group decides whether to continue using the innovation and to what extent.

Rogers noted that the innovation process is influenced both by the individuals involved in the process and by the innovation itself. Individuals include innovators, early adopters of the innovation, the early majority (who deliberate longer than early adopters and then take action), late adopters, and "laggards" who resist change and are often critical of others willing to accept the innovation.

According to Rogers, the characteristics that affect the likelihood that an innovation will be adopted include (1) its perceived relative advantage over other strategies, (2) its compatibility with existing norms and beliefs, (3) the degree of complexity involved in adopting the innovation, (4) the "trialability" of the innovation (i.e., the extent to which it can be tested on a trial basis), and (5) the observability of the results. Greenhalgh et al. (2004) expanded upon these characteristics of an innovation, adding (1) the potential for reinvention, (2) how flexibly the innovation can be used, (3) the perceived risk of adoption, (4) the presence of a clear potential for improved performance, (5) the knowledge required to adopt the innovation, and (6) the technical support required.

Awareness of the stages of diffusion, the differing responses to innovations, and the characteristics that promote adoption can help engagement leaders match strategies to the readiness of stakeholders. For example, a community-engaged health promotion campaign might include raising awareness about the severity of a health problem (knowledge, the first stage in Rogers' scheme), transforming awareness into concern for the problem (persuasion), establishing a community-wide intervention initiative (adoption), developing the necessary infrastructure so that the provision of services remains extensive and constant in reaching residents (implementation), and/or evaluation of the project (confirmation).

Awareness of the stages of diffusion, the differing responses to innovations, and the characteristics that promote adoption can help engagement leaders match strategies to the readiness of stakeholders.

Community-Based Participatory Research

Community-based participatory research (CBPR) is the most well-known framework for CEnR. As a highly evolved collaborative approach, CBPR would be represented on the right side of the continuum shown in Figure 1.1 (page 8). In CBPR, all collaborators respect the strengths that each brings to the partnership, and the community participates fully in all aspects of the research process. Although CBPR begins with an important research topic, its aim is to achieve social change to improve health outcomes and eliminate health disparities (Israel et al., 2003).

Wallerstein et al. (2008) conducted a two-year pilot study that looked at how the CBPR process influences or predicts outcomes. Using Internet survey methods and existing published literature, the study focused on two questions: *What*

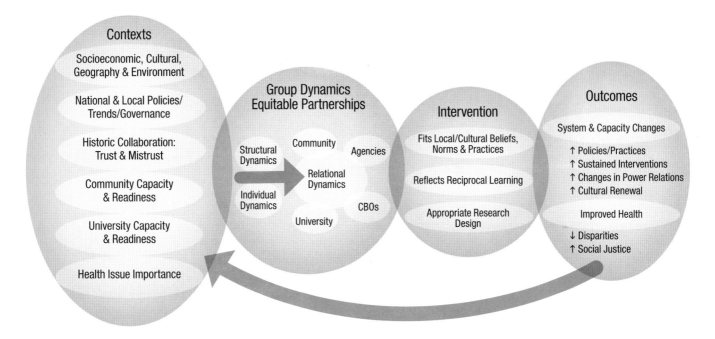

Contexts	Group Dynamics		Intervention	Outcomes

• Social-economic, cultural, geographic, political-historical, environmental factors	**Structural Dynamics**
	• Diversity
	• Complexity
	• Formal agreements
	• Real power/resource sharing
	• Alignment with CBPR principles
	• Length of time in partnership
		Relational Dynamics
		• Safety
		• Dialogue, listening & mutual learning
		• Leadership & stewardship
		• Influence & power dynamics
		• Flexibility
		• Self & collective reflection
		• Participatory decision-making & negotiation
		• Integration of local beliefs to group process
		• Flexibility
		• Task roles & communication
			• Intervention adapted or created within local culture
			
			• Intervention informed by local settings and organizations
			
			• Shared learning between academic and community knowledge
			
			• Research and evaluation design reflects partnership input
			
			• Bidirectional translation, implementation & dissemination
				CBPR System & Capacity Changes
				• Changes in policies/ practices:
				  - In universities and communities
				
				• Culturally based & sustainable interventions
				
				• Changes in power relations
				
				• Empowerment:
				  - Community voices heard
				
				  - Capacities of advisory councils
				
				  - Critical thinking
				
				• Cultural revitalization & renewal
				
				Health Outcomes
				• Transformed social/economic conditions
				
				• Reduced health disparities

• Policies/Trends: National/ local governance & political climate				
• Historic degree of collaboration and trust between university & community				
• Community: capacity, readiness & experience	**Individual Dynamics** • Core values • Motivations for participating • Personal relationships • Cultural identities/ humility • Bridge people on research team • Individual beliefs, spirituality & meaning • Community reputation of PI			
• University: capacity, readiness & reputation				
• Perceived severity of health issues				

Used with permission from Minkler et al., 2008.

Figure 1.3. CBPR Conceptual Model. A later version of this diagram can be found in Wallerstein et al. (2010)

is the added value of CBPR to the research itself and to producing outcomes? What are the potential pathways to intermediate system and capacity change outcomes and to more distal health outcomes? Through a consensus process using a national advisory committee, the authors formed a conceptual logic model of CBPR processes leading to outcomes (Figure 1.3). The model addresses four dimensions of CBPR and outlines the potential relationships between each. The authors identify:

> "contextual factors" that shape the nature of the research and the part-
> nership, and can determine whether and how a partnership is initiated.
> Next, group dynamics…interact with contextual factors to produce the
> intervention and its research design. Finally, intermediate system and
> capacity changes, and ultimately, health outcomes, result directly from
> the intervention research (p. 380).

Models such as these are essential to efforts to empirically assess or evaluate community engagement practices and disseminate effective approaches.

Translational Research

NIH has created a new impetus toward participatory research through an increase in funding mechanisms that require participation and through its current focus on "translation" (i.e., turning research into practice by taking it from "the bench to the bedside and into the community"). Increasingly, community participation is recognized as necessary for translating existing research to implement and sustain new health promotion programs, change clinical practice, improve population health, and reduce health disparities. The CTSA initiative is the primary example of an NIH-funded mechanism requiring a translational approach to the clinical research enterprise (Horowitz et al., 2009).

The components of translational research are understood differently by different authors in the field. In one widely used schema, translational research is separated into four segments: T1–T4 (Kon, 2008). T1 represents the translation of basic science into clinical research (phase 1 and 2 clinical trials), T2 represents the further research that establishes relevance to patients (phase 3 trials), T3 is translation into clinical practice, and T4 is the movement of "scientific knowledge into the public sector… thereby changing people's everyday lives" (p. 59) through public and other policy changes.

Westfall et al. (2007) have identified the lack of successful collaboration between community physicians and academic researchers as one of the major roadblocks to translation. They note that although the majority of patients receive most of their medical care from a physician in a community setting, most clinical research takes place in an academic setting (Westfall et al., 2007). Consequently, the results of clinical trials may not be easily generalized to real-world clinical practices.

One solution to this dilemma is practice-based research (PBR): engaging the practice community in research. PBR has traditionally been conducted in a primary care setting using a coordinated infrastructure (physicians, nurses, and office staff), although the recent emphasis on translation has contributed to the emergence of more specialized practice-based research networks (e.g., in nursing, dental care, and pharmacy). Like all efforts in engagement, developing PBR includes building trust, sharing decision making, and recognizing the expertise of all partners. PBR addresses three particular concerns about clinical practice: identifying medical directives that, despite recommendations, are not being implemented; validating the effectiveness of clinical interventions in community-based primary care settings; and increasing the number of patients participating in evidence-based treatments (Westfall et al., 2007). "PBR also provides the laboratory for a range of research approaches that are sometimes better suited to translational research than are clinical trials: observational studies, physician and patient surveys, secondary data analysis, and qualitative research" (Westfall et al., 2007, p. 405).

> Like all efforts in engagement, developing PBR includes building trust, sharing decision making, and recognizing the expertise of all partners.

CONCLUSION

The wide-ranging literature summarized above shares several major themes:

- There are multiple reasons for community-engaged health promotion and research.

- Community engagement must be conducted in a manner that is respectful of all partners and mindful of their need to benefit from collaboration.

- It is important to understand context (in all its complexity) as it affects health problems and the development of health solutions.

- We must recognize that community-engaged health improvement is a long-term, evolving process.

Chapter 2 covers nine principles of community engagement that are grounded in the preceding literature. Succeeding chapters develop practical applications and examples of the issues discussed in the first two chapters, specifically in the areas of planning and implementing CEnR and health promotion (Chapters 3 and 5), creating the management and organizational support necessary for community engagement (Chapter 4), using social networking for community engagement (Chapter 6), and evaluating community-engaged projects (Chapter 7).

REFERENCES

Airhihenbuwa CO. *Health and culture: beyond the western paradigm.* Thousand Oaks (CA): Sage; 1995.

Airhihenbuwa CO. On being comfortable with being uncomfortable: centering an Africanist vision in our gateway to global health. *Health Education and Behavior* 2007;34(1):31-42.

Alinsky SD. *Citizen participation and community organization in planning and urban renewal.* Chicago: Industrial Areas Foundation; 1962.

Blumenthal DS. A community coalition board creates a set of values for community-based research. *Preventing Chronic Disease* 2006;3(1):A16.

Blumenthal DS, DiClemente RJ (editors). *Community-based health research: issues and methods.* New York: Springer; 2004.

Braithwaite RL, Bianchi C, Taylor SE. Ethnographic approach to community organization and health empowerment. *Health Education Quarterly* 1994;21(3):407-416.

Brown P, Morello-Frosch R, Green Brody J, Gasior Altman R, Rudel RA, Senier L, et al. *IRB challenges in multi-partner community-based participatory research.* Research Ethics and Environmental Health; 2006. Retrieved from http://www.researchethics.org/uploads/pdf/x-IRB-paper%206-16-07%20rev.pdf.

Brugge D, Cole A. A case study of community-based participatory research ethics: the Healthy Public Housing Initiative. *Science and Engineering Ethics* 2003;9(4):485-501.

Butterfoss FD. Process evaluation for community participation. *Annual Review of Public Health* 2006;27:323-340.

Butterfoss FD, Goodman RM, Wandersman A. Community coalitions for health promotion and disease prevention. *Health Education Research* 1993;8(3):315-330.

Butterfoss FD, Kegler MC. (2002). Toward a comprehensive understanding of community coalitions. In: DiClemente RJ, Crosby RA, Kegler MC (editors). *Emerging theories in health promotion practice and research: strategies for improving public health* (1st ed., pp. 157-193). San Francisco: Jossey-Bass; 2002.

CARE: Community Alliance for Research and Engagement. *Principles and guidelines for community-university research partnerships.* New Haven (CT): Yale University; 2009.

Carpenter-Song EA, Nordquest Schwallie M, Longhofer J. Cultural competence reexamined: critique and directions for the future. *Psychiatric Services* 2007;58, (10):1362-1365.

Centers for Disease Control and Prevention. *Principles of community engagement* (1st ed.). Atlanta (GA): CDC/ATSDR Committee on Community Engagement; 1997.

Centers for Disease Control and Prevention. The social-ecological model: a framework for prevention. Atlanta (GA): Centers for Disease Control and Prevention; 2007. Retrieved from http://www.cdc.gov/ncipc/dvp/social-eco-logical-model_DVP.htm.

Center for Advanced Study. Improving the system for protecting human subjects: counteracting IRB "mission creep." University of Illinois Law & Economics Research Paper No. LE06-016. Urbana-Champaign: University of Illinois; 2004.

Chávez V, Duran B, Baker QE, Avila MM, Wallerstein N. The dance of race and privilege in CBPR. In: Minkler M, Wallerstein N (editors). *Community-based participatory research for health* (2nd ed., pp. 91-103). San Francisco: Jossey-Bass; 2008.

Chávez V, Minkler M, Wallerstein N, Spencer MS. Community organizing for health and social justice. In: Cohen L, Chávez V, Chehimi S (editors). *Prevention is primary: strategies for community well-being* (1st ed., pp. 95-120). San Francisco: John Wiley and Sons; 2007.

Chen DT, Jones L, Gelberg L. Ethics of clinical research within a community-academic partnered participatory framework. *Ethnicity & Disease* 2006;16(1 Suppl 1):S118-135.

Cohen L, Baer N, Satterwhite P. Developing effective coalitions: an eight step guide. In: Wurzbach ME (editor). *Community health education and promotion: A guide to program design and evaluation* (2nd ed., pp. 144-161). Gaithersburg (MD): Aspen; 2002.

Dévieux JG, Malow RM, Rosenberg R, Jean-Gilles M, Samuels D, Ergon-Pérez E, et al. Cultural adaptation in translational research: field experiences. *Journal of Urban Health Bulletin of the New York Academy of Medicine* 2005;82(2 Suppl 3):iii82-i91.

Doll LS, Bonzo SE, Mercy JA, Sleet DA, Haas EN. *Handbook of injury and violence prevention* (2nd ed.). Atlanta (GA): Springer; 2008.

Emanuel EJ, Wendler D, Grady C. What makes clinical research ethical? *JAMA* 2000;283:2701-2711.

Eng E, Parker E. Measuring community competence in the Mississippi Delta: the interface between program evaluation and empowerment. *Health Education and Behavior* 1994;21(2):199-220.

Fawcett SB, Paine-Andrews A, Fancisco VT, Schultz JA, Richter KP, Berkley-Patton J, et al. Evaluating community initiatives for health and development. In: Rootman I, McQueen D (editors). *Evaluating health promotion approaches* (pp. 241-277). Copenhagen, Denmark: World Health Organization; 1995.

Fisher EB, Brownson CA, O'Toole ML, Shetty G, Anwuri VV, Fazzone P, et al. The Robert Wood Johnson Foundation Diabetes Initiative: demonstration projects emphasizing self-management. *The Diabetes Educator* 2007;33(1):83-84,86-88,91-92,passim.

Flavian C, Guinaliu M. The influence of virtual communities on distribution strategies in the internet. *International Journal of Retail & Distribution Management* 2005;33(6):405-425.

Flicker S, Travers R, Guta A, McDonald S, Meagher A. Ethical dilemmas in community-based participatory research: recommendations for institutional review boards. *Journal of Urban Health* 2007;84(4):478-493.

Freire P. *Pedagogy of the oppressed.* New York: Herder and Herder; 1970.

Gbadegesin S, Wendler D. Protecting communities in health research from exploitation. *Bioethics* 2006;20(5):248-253.

Geiger H. Community health centers: health care as an instrument of social change. In: Sidel VW, Sidel R (editors). *Reforming medicine: lessons of the last quarter century* (pp. 11–32). New York: Pantheon Books; 1984.

Gilbert SG. Supplementing the traditional institutional review board with an environmental health and community review board. *Environmental Health Perspectives* 2006;114(10):1626-1629.

Green L, Daniel M, Novick L. Partnerships and coalitions for community-based research. *Public Health Reports* 2001a;116(Suppl 1):20-31.

Green LW, Mercer SL. Can public health researchers and agencies reconcile the push from funding bodies and the pull from communities? *American Journal of Public Health* 2001b;91(12):1926-1929.

Greenhalgh T, Robert G, Macfarlane F, Bate P, Kyriakidou O. Diffusion of innovations in service organizations: systematic review and recommendations. *Milbank Quarterly* 2004;82(4):581-629.

Hahn RA (editor). *Anthropology in public health.* New York: Oxford University; 1999.

Hanson P. Citizen involvement in community health promotion: a role application of CDC's PATCH model. *International Quarterly of Community Health Education* 1988;9(3):177-186.

Harrell SP, Bond MA. Listening to diversity stories: principles for practice in community research and action. *American Journal of Community Psychology* 2006;37(3-4):365-376.

Hatcher MT, Nicola RM. Building constituencies for public health. In: Novick LF, Morrow CB, Mays GP (editors). *Public health administration: principles for population-based management* (2nd ed., pp. 443-458). Sudbury (MA): Jones and Bartlett; 2008.

Henry SG. The tyranny of reality. *JAMA* 2011;305(4):338-339.

Hill A, De Zapien JG, Staten LK, McClelland DJ, Garza R, Moore-Monroy M, et al. From program to policy: expanding the role of community coalitions. *Preventing Chronic Disease* 2007; 4(4):A103.

Horowitz CR, Robinson M, Seifer S. Community-based participatory research from the margin to the mainstream: are researchers prepared? *Circulation* 2009;119(19):2633.

Hur MH. Empowerment in terms of theoretical perspectives: exploring a typology of the process and components across disciplines. *Journal of Community Psychology* 2006;34(5):523.

Institute of Medicine. *The future of public health.* Washington (DC): National Academy Press; 1988.

Israel BA, Schulz AJ, Parker EA, Becker AB. Review of community-based research: assessing partnership approaches to improve public health. *Annual Review of Public Health* 1988;192:173-202.

Israel BA, Schulz AJ, Parker EA, Becker AB, Allen AJ, Guzman JR. Critical issues in developing and following community based participatory research principles. In: Minkler M, Wallerstein N (editors). *Community-based participatory research for health* (pp. 53-76). San Francisco: Jossey-Bass; 2003.

Iton T. Transforming public health practice to achieve health equity. Paper presented at the Health Trust Health Equities Summit, February 4, 2009, San Jose, CA. Retrieved from http://www.healthtrust.org/Health%20Equity%20 Summit%20-%20Dr.%20Anthony%20Iton.pdf.

James W. The consciousness of self. *The principles of psychology.* New York: Holt; 1890.

Jones MR, Horner RD, Edwards LJ, Hoff J, Armstrong SB, Smith-Hammond CA, et al. Racial variation in initial stroke severity. *Stroke* 2000;31(3):563-567.

Khanlou N, Peter E. Participatory action research: considerations for ethical review. *Social Science & Medicine* 2005;60(10):2333-2340.

Kiefer CW. *Doing health anthropology: research methods for community assessment and change* (1st ed.). New York: Springer; 2007.

Kleinman A. *Patients and healers in the context of culture* (vol. 3). Berkeley (CA): University of California; 1980.

Kleinman A, Benson P. Anthropology in the clinic: the problem of cultural competency and how to fix it. *PLoS Medicine* 2006;3(10):e294.

Kon AA. The Clinical and Translational Science Award (CTSA) Consortium and the translational research model. *American Journal of Bioethics* 2008;8(3):58-60,W51-53.

Kozinets RV. The field behind the screen: using netnography for marketing research in online communities. *Journal of Marketing Research* 2002;39(1):61-72.

Kretzmann JP, McKnight JL. *A guide to mapping and mobilizing the economic capacities of local residents.* Evanston (IL): Department of Economics and Center for Urban Affairs and Policy Research; 1996.

Krieger N, Williams D, Zierler S. "Whiting out" white privilege will not advance the study of how racism harms health. *American Journal of Public Health* 1999;89(5):782-783.

Krug E, Dahlberg L. Violence—a global public health problem. In: Krug E, Dahlberg L, Mercy J, Zwi A, Lozano R (editors). *World report on violence and health* (pp. 1-56). Geneva, Switzerland: World Health Organization; 2002.

Krumeich A, Weijts W, Reddy P, Meijer-Weitz A. The benefits of anthropological approaches for health promotion research and practice. *Health Education Research* 2001;16(2):121-130.

Kumagai AK, Lypson ML. Beyond cultural competence: critical consciousness, social justice, and multicultural education. *Academic Medicine* 2009;84(6):782-787.

Labonte R, Robertson A. Delivering the goods, showing our stuff: the case for a constructivist paradigm for health promotion research and practice. *Health Education Quarterly* 1996;23(4):431-447.

Levine RJ. *Ethics and the regulation of clinical research* (2nd ed.). New Haven (CT): Yale University; 1988.

Levine S, White P. Exchange as a conceptual framework for the study of inter-organizational relationships. *Administrative Science Quarterly* 1961;5(4):583-601.

Malone RE, Yerger VB, McGruder C, Froelicher E. "It's like Tuskegee in reverse": a case study of ethical tensions in institutional review board review of community-based participatory research. *American Journal of Public Health* 2006;96(11):1914-1919.

Maton KI. Empowering community settings: agents of individual development, community betterment, and positive social change. *American Journal of Community Psychology* 2008;41(1):4-21.

Michener JL, Yaggy S, Lyn M, Warburton S, Champagne M, Black M, et al. Improving the health of the community: Duke's experience with community engagement. *Academic Medicine* 2008;83(4):408-413.

Miller RL, Shinn M. Learning from communities: overcoming difficulties in dissemination of prevention and promotion efforts. *American Journal of Community Psychology* 2005;35(3-4):169-183.

Minkler M. Improving health through community organization. In: Glanz K, Lewis FM, Rimer BK (editors). *Health behavior and health education: theory, research and practice* (pp. 169-181). San Francisco: Jossey-Bass; 1990.

Minkler M. Ethical challenges for the "outside" researcher in community-based participatory research. *Health Education and Behavior* 2004;31(6):684-697.

Minkler M. *Community organizing and community building for health* (2nd ed.). Piscataway (NJ): Rutgers University; 2004.

Minkler M, Pies C. Ethical Issues in community organization and community participation. In: Minkler M (editor). *Community organizing and community building for health* (1st ed., pp. 116-133). Piscataway (NJ): Rutgers University; 1997.

Minkler M, Wallerstein N. Improving health through community organization. In: Minkler M (editor). *Community organizing and community building for health* (2nd ed., pp. 26-50). Piscataway (NJ): Rutgers University; 2004.

Minkler M, Wallerstein N (editors). *Community-based participatory research for health: from process to outcomes* (2nd ed.). San Francisco: Jossey-Bass; 2008.

Minkler M, Wallerstein N. Community-based participatory research for health: from process to outcomes. *Health Promotion Practice* 2009;10(3):317-318.

Nyswander D. Education for health: some principles and their applications. *Health Education Monographs* 1956;14:65-70.

Putnam R. *Bowling alone: the collapse and revival of American community.* New York: Simon and Schuster; 2001.

Quinn SC. Ethics in public health research: protecting human subjects: the role of community advisory boards. *American Journal of Public Health* 2004;94(6):918-922.

Resnicow K, Baranowski T, Ahluwalia JS, Braithwaite RL. Cultural sensitivity in public health: defined and demystified. *Ethnicity & Disease* 1999;9(1):10-21.

Rheingold H. *The virtual community: homesteading on the electronic frontier.* Cambridge (MA): Massachusetts Institute of Technology; 2000.

Rich RC, Edelstein M, Hallman WK, Wandersman AH. Citizen participation and empowerment: the case of local environmental hazards. *American Journal of Community Psychology* 1995;23(5):657-676.

Ridings CM, Gefen D, Arinze B. Some antecedents and effects of trust in virtual communities. *Journal of Strategic Information Systems* 2002;11(3-4):271-295.

Rogers E. *Diffusion of innovations* (4th ed.). New York: Free Press; 1995.

Ross LF, Loup A, Nelson RM, Botkin JR, Kost R, Smith GR, et al. The challenges of collaboration for academic and community partners in a research partnership: points to consider. *Journal of Empirical Research on Human Research Ethics* 2010a;5(1):19-31.

Ross LF, Loup A, Nelson RM, Botkin JR, Kost R, Smith GR, et al. Nine key functions for a human subjects protection program for community-engaged research: points to consider. *Journal of Empirical Research on Human Research Ethics* 2010b;5(1):33-47.

Ross LF, Loup A, Nelson RM, Botkin JR, Kost R, Smith GR Jr, et al. Human subjects protections in community-engaged research: a research ethics framework. *Journal of Empirical Research on Human Research Ethics* 2010c;5(1):5-17.

Russell N, Igras S, Kuoh H, Pavin M, Wickerstrom J. *The active community engagement continuum.* ACQUIRE Project Working Paper. 2008. Retrieved from http://www.acquireproject.org/fileadmin/user_upload/ACQUIRE/Publications/ACE-Working-Paper-final.pdf.

Sallis JF, Owen N, Fisher EB. Ecological models of health behavior. In: Glanz K, Rimer BK, Viswanath K (editors). *Health behavior and health education* (4th ed., pp. 465-485). San Francisco: John Wiley & Sons; 2008.

Scholle SH, Torda P, Peikes D, Han E, Genevro J. Engaging patients and families in the medical home. AHRQ Publication No. 10-0083-EF. Rockville (MD): Agency for Healthcare Research and Quality; 2010.

Shalowitz M, Isacco A, Barquin N, Clark-Kauffman E, Delger P, Nelson D, et al. Community-based participatory research: a review of the literature with strategies for community engagement. *Journal of Developmental and Behavioral Pediatrics* 2009;30(4):350-361.

Shore N. Re-conceptualizing the Belmont Report: a community-based participatory research perspective. *Journal of Community Practice* 2006;14(4):5-26.

Shore N. Community-based participatory research and the ethics review process. *Journal of Empirical Research on Human Research Ethics* 2007;2(1):31-41.

Shoultz J, Oneha MF, Magnussen L, Hla MM, Brees-Saunders Z, Cruz MD, et al. Finding solutions to challenges faced in community-based participatory research between academic and community organizations. *Journal of Interprofessional Care* 2006;20(2):133-144.

Silka L, Cleghorn GD, Grullón M, Tellez T. Creating community-based participatory research in a diverse community: a case study. *Journal of Empirical Research on Human Research Ethics* 2008;3(2):5-16.

Silverstein M, Banks M, Fish S, Bauchner H. Variability in institutional approaches to ethics review of community-based research conducted in collaboration with unaffiliated organizations. *Journal of Empirical Research on Human Research Ethics* 2008;3(2):69-76.

Sofaer S. *Coalitions and public health: a program manager's guide to the issues.* Washington (DC): Academy for Educational Development; 1993.

Staley K. *Exploring impact: public involvement in NHS, public health and social care research.* Eastleigh, United Kingdom: INVOLVE; 2009.

Stokols D. Translating social ecological theory into guidelines for community health promotion. *American Journal of Health Promotion* 1996;10(4):282-298.

Sullivan M, Kone A, Senturia KD, Chrisman NJ, Ciske SJ, Krieger JW. Researcher and researched—community perspectives: toward bridging the gap. *Health Education and Behavior* 2001;28(2):130-149.

Thompson B, Kinne S. Social change theory: applications to community health. In: Bracht N (editor). *Health promotion at the community level* (1st ed., pp. 45-65). Newbury Park (CA): Sage; 1990.

Viswanathan M, Ammerman A, Eng E, Gartlehner G, Lohr KN, Griffith D, et al. *Community-based participatory research: assessing the evidence.* AHRQ Publication No. 04-E022-2. Rockville (MD): Agency for Healthcare Research and Quality; 2004.

Wallerstein N. Empowerment to reduce health disparities. *Scandinavian Journal of Public Health Supplement* 2002;59:72-77.

Wallerstein N, Duran B. The conceptual, historical and practice roots of community-based participatory research and related participatory traditions. In: Minkler M, Wallerstein N (editors). *Community-based participatory research for health* (1st ed., pp. 27-52). San Francisco: Jossey-Bass; 2003.

Wallerstein NB, Duran B. Using community-based participatory research to address health disparities. *Health Promotion Practice* 2006;7(3):312-323.

Wallerstein N, Duran B. Community-based participatory research contributions to intervention research: the intersection of science and practice to improve health equity. *American Journal of Public Health* 2010;100(Suppl 1):S40-46.

Wallerstein N, Oetzel J, Duran B, Tafoya G, Belone L, Rae R. What predicts outcomes in CBPR? In: Minkler M, Wallerstein N (editors). *Community-based participatory research for health: from process to outcomes* (2nd ed., pp. 371-392). San Francisco: Jossey-Bass; 2008.

Wandersman A, Florin P, Friedmann R, Meier R. *Who participates, who does not, and why? An analysis of voluntary neighborhood organizations in the United States and Israel.* New York: Springer; 1987.

Westfall JM, Mold J, Fagnan L. Practice-based research—"Blue Highways" on the NIH roadmap. *JAMA* 2007;297(4):403-406.

Williams RL, Shelley BM, Sussman AL. The marriage of community-based participatory research and practice-based research networks: can it work? A Research Involving Outpatient Settings Network (RIOS Net) study. *Journal of the American Board of Family Medicine* 2009;22(4):428-435.

Wing S. Social responsibility and research ethics in community-driven studies of industrialized hog production. *Environmental Health Perspectives* 2002;110(5):437-444.

World Health Organization. *Constitution.* New York: WHO; 1947.

Yale Center for Clinical Investigation/Community Alliance for Research and Engagement. B*eyond scientific publication: strategies for disseminating research findings.* New Haven (CT): Yale University; 2009.

Yonas MA, Jones N, Eng E, Vines AI, Aronson R, Griffith DM, et al. The art and science of integrating Undoing Racism with CBPR: challenges of pursuing NIH funding to investigate cancer care and racial equity. *Journal of Urban Health* 2006;83(6):1004-1012.

Zakocs RC, Edwards EM. What explains community coalition effectiveness? A review of the literature. *American Journal of Preventive Medicine* 2006;30(4):351-361.

Principles of Community Engagement

Chapter 2
Principles of Community Engagement[1]

INTRODUCTION

In developing this primer, the authors drew on their knowledge of the literature, their practice experiences, and the collective experience of their constituencies in the practice of community engagement. These practical experiences, combined with the organizing concepts, models, and frameworks from the literature, which were discussed in Chapter 1, suggested several underlying principles that can assist health professionals, researchers, policy makers, and community leaders in planning, designing, implementing, and evaluating community engagement efforts. Because community processes can be complex, challenging, and labor-intensive, however, these health professionals and others require dedicated resources to help ensure their success. In addition, efforts to engage communities require skill sets that leaders may not have previously developed. Thoughtful consideration of the nine principles laid out in this chapter and what is needed to put them into action will help readers to form effective partnerships. The principles are organized in three sections: items to consider prior to beginning engagement, what is necessary for engagement to occur, and what to consider for engagement to be

[1] This chapter was adapted from the first edition of *Principles of Community Engagement.*

successful. Each principle covers a broad practice area of engagement, often addressing multiple issues.

BEFORE STARTING A COMMUNITY ENGAGEMENT EFFORT...

1. Be clear about the purposes or goals of the engagement effort and the populations and/or communities you want to engage.

Those wishing to engage the community need to be able to communicate to that community why its participation is worthwhile. Of course, as seen in the discussion about coalition building and community organizing in Chapter 1, simply being able to articulate that involvement is worthwhile does not guarantee participation. Those implementing the effort should be prepared for a variety of responses from the community. There may be many barriers to engagement and, as discussed in Chapter 1's section on community participation, appropriate compensation should be provided to participants. The processes for involvement and participation must be appropriate for meeting the overall goals and objectives of the engagement.

The impetus for specific engagement efforts may vary. For example, legislation or policy may make community involvement a condition of funding. Engagement leaders may see community organizing and mobilization as part of their mission or profession, or they may recognize the strengths of community engagement: its potential to enhance the ethical foundations of action, the identification of issues, the design and delivery of programs, and translational research. Alternatively, outside pressures may demand that an entity be more responsive to community concerns.

Just as the impetus for community engagement varies, so do its goals. For example, efforts in community engagement could be focused on specific health issues, such as HIV/AIDS, tuberculosis, mental illness, substance abuse, immunizations, or cardiovascular disease. Alternatively, efforts could have a very broad focus, as in the following examples:

- Focus on overall community improvement, including economic and infrastructure development, which will directly or indirectly contribute to health improvements and disease prevention.

- Ask community members to specify their health-related concerns, identify areas that need action, and become involved in planning, designing, implementing, and evaluating appropriate programs.

The level at which goals are focused has implications for managing and sustaining the engagement. A broader goal may enable community leaders to involve larger segments of the community, whereas a narrower focus may keep activities more directed and manageable.

Similarly, participation by the community could have several possible dimensions. Broadly speaking, leaders of efforts to engage communities need to be clear about whether they are (1) seeking data, information, advice, and feedback to help them design programs, or (2) interested in partnering and sharing control with the community. The latter includes being willing to address the issues that the community identifies as important, even if those are not the ones originally anticipated.

It is equally important to be clear about who is to be engaged, at least initially. Is it all those who reside within certain geographic boundaries? Or is it a specific racial/ethnic group, an income-specific population, or an age group, such as youth? Is it a specific set of institutions and groups, such as faith communities, schools, or the judicial system? Or is it a combination? Is it a "virtual" community sharing a common interest? How might other collaborations or partnerships in the community of interest enhance engagement efforts? Answers to these questions will begin to provide the parameters for the engagement effort.

2. Become knowledgeable about the community's culture, economic conditions, social networks, political and power structures, norms and values, demographic trends, history, and experience with efforts by outside groups to engage it in various programs. Learn about the community's perceptions of those initiating the engagement activities.

It is important to learn as much about the community as possible, through both qualitative and quantitative methods, and from as many sources as feasible. Many of the organizing concepts, models, and frameworks presented in Chapter 1 support this principle. Social ecological theories, for example, emphasize the need to understand the larger physical and social/

cultural environment and its interaction with individual health behaviors. An understanding of how the community perceives the benefits and costs of participating will facilitate decision making and consensus building and will translate into improved program planning, design, policy development, organization, and advocacy. The concept of stages of diffusion of innovation (discussed in Chapter 1) highlights the need to assess the community's readiness to adopt new strategies. Understanding the community will help leaders in the engagement effort to map community assets, develop a picture of how business is done, and identify the individuals and groups whose support is necessary, including which individuals or groups must be approached and involved in the initial stages of engagement.

Many communities are already involved in coalitions and partnerships developed around specific issues such as HIV/AIDS, the prevention of substance abuse, and community and economic development. It is important to consider how attempts to engage or mobilize the community around new issues may affect these preexisting efforts.

It is also helpful for those initiating the community engagement process to consider how the community perceives them (or their affiliations). Understanding these perceptions will help them identify strengths they can build upon and barriers they need to overcome. There are many community-engagement techniques that can be used to (1) learn about the community's perceptions of the credibility of those initiating the process and (2) simultaneously lay the groundwork for meaningful and genuine partnerships.

FOR ENGAGEMENT TO OCCUR, IT IS NECESSARY TO...

3. Go to the community, establish relationships, build trust, work with the formal and informal leadership, and seek commitment from community organizations and leaders to create processes for mobilizing the community.

Engagement is based on community support. The literature on community participation and organization discussed in Chapter 1 illuminates this principle and suggests that positive change is more likely to occur when community members are an integral part of a program's development and implementation. All partners must be actively respected from the start. For example, meeting with key community leaders and groups in their surroundings helps to build trust for a true partnership. Such meetings provide the organizers of engage-ment activities with more information about the community, its concerns, and the factors that will facilitate or constrain participation. In addition, commu-nity members need to see and experience "real" benefits for the extra time, effort, and involvement they are asked to give. Once a successful rapport is established, meetings and exchanges with community members can build into an ongoing and substantive partnership.

When contacting the community, some engagement leaders find it most effective to reach out to the fullest possible range of formal and informal leaders and organizations. They try to work with all factions, expand the engagement table, and avoid becoming iden-tified with one group. Coalition building, as described in Chapter 1, can be a key part of community engagement. Alternatively, implementers of engagement efforts may find that identifying and working primarily with key stakeholders is the most successful approach. Therefore, they engage with a smaller, perhaps more manageable, number of community members to achieve their mission. The range of individuals and groups contacted for an engagement effort depends in part on the issue at hand, the engagement strategy chosen, and whether the effort is mandated or voluntary.

When contacting the community, some engagement leaders find it most effective to reach out to the fullest possible range of formal and informal leaders and organizations.

It is essential for those engaging a community to adhere to the highest ethical standards. Indeed, under some circumstances, community engagement might itself be considered an ethical imperative. The rights, interests, and well-being of individuals and communities must have the utmost priority. Past ethical failures such as the Tuskegee syphilis study have created distrust among some communities and have produced great challenges for community organizers. The community must be educated about any potential for harm through its involvement with or endorsement of an initiative so it can make an informed decision. Failure to act ethically is not an option.

4. Remember and accept that collective self-determination is the responsibility and right of all people in a community. No external entity should assume it can bestow on a community the power to act in its own self-interest.

Just because an institution or organization introduces itself into the community does not mean that it automatically becomes of the community. An organization is of the community when it is controlled by individuals or groups who are members of the community. This concept of self-determination is central to the concept of community empowerment. The dynamic can be quite complex, however, because communities themselves may have factions that contend for power and influence. More broadly, it should be recognized that internal and external forces may be at play in any engagement effort. As addressed in Principle 6 (below), a diversity of ideas may be encountered and negotiated throughout the engagement process.

The literature on community empowerment strongly supports the idea that problems and potential solutions should be defined by the community. Communities and individuals need to "own" the issues, name the problem, identify action areas, plan and implement strategies, and evaluate outcomes. Moreover, people in a community are more likely to become involved if they identify with the issues being addressed, consider them important, and feel they have influence and can make a contribution. Participation will also be easier to elicit if people encounter few barriers to participation, consider the benefits of participating to outweigh the costs (e.g., time, energy, dollars), and believe that the participation process and related organizational climate are open and supportive.

FOR ENGAGEMENT TO SUCCEED...

5. Partnering with the community is necessary to create change and improve health.

The American Heritage Dictionary defines partnership as "a relationship between individuals or groups that is characterized by mutual cooperation and responsibility, as for the achievement of a specified goal." Many of the organizing concepts, models, and frameworks highlighted in Chapter 1, such as social ecology, community participation, and community organization, speak to the relationship between community partnerships and positive change. Indeed, community-based participatory research and current approaches to translational research explicitly recognize that community engagement significantly enhances the potential for research to lead to improved health by improving participation in the research, its implementation, and dissemination of its findings. Community engagement based on improving health takes place in the context of and must respond to economic, social, and political trends that affect health and health disparities. Furthermore, as the literature on community empowerment contends, equitable community partnerships and transparent discussions of power are more likely to lead to desired outcomes (see Principle 4). The individuals and groups involved in a partnership must identify opportunities for co-learning and feel that they each have something meaningful to contribute to the pursuit of improved health, while at the same time seeing something to gain. Every party in such a relationship also holds important responsibility for the final outcome of an effort.

6. All aspects of community engagement must recognize and respect the diversity of the community. Awareness of the various cultures of a community and other factors affecting diversity must be paramount in planning, designing, and implementing approaches to engaging a community.

Diversity may be related to economic, educational, employment, or health status as well as differences in culture, language, race, ethnicity, age, gender, mobility, literacy, or personal interests. These elements of diversity may affect individuals' and communities' access to health care delivery, their health status, and their response to community engagement efforts. For example, as indicated in Chapter 1, the processes, strategies, and techniques used to engage the community must be respectful of and complement cultural traditions. The systems perspective suggests attention to another element of community diversity: the diversity of roles that different people and organizations play in the functioning of a community. Engaging these diverse populations will require the use of multiple engagement strategies.

7. Community engagement can only be sustained by identifying and mobilizing community assets and strengths and by developing the community's capacity and resources to make decisions and take action.

Community assets include the interests, skills, and experiences of individuals and local organizations as well as the networks of relationships that connect them. Individual and institutional resources such as facilities, materials, skills, and economic power all can be mobilized for community health decision making and action. In brief, community members and institutions should be viewed as resources to bring about change and take action. The discussion of community participation in Chapter 1 highlights the need to offer an exchange of resources to ensure community participation. Of course, depending on the "trigger" for the engagement process (e.g., a funded mandate vs. a more grassroots effort), resources are likely to be quite varied.

Although it is essential to begin by using existing resources, the literature on capacity building and coalitions stresses that engagement is more likely to be sustained when new resources and capacities are developed. Engaging the community in making decisions about health and taking action in that arena may involve the provision of experts and resources to help communities develop the necessary capacities (e.g., through leadership training) and infrastructure to analyze situations, make decisions, and take action.

8. Organizations that wish to engage a community as well as individuals seeking to effect change must be prepared to release control of actions or interventions to the community and be flexible enough to meet its changing needs.

Engaging the community is ultimately about facilitating community-driven action (see discussions under community empowerment and community organization in Chapter 1). Community action should include the many elements of a community that are needed for the action to be sustained while still creating a manageable process. Community engagement will create changes in relationships and in the way institutions and individuals demonstrate their capacity and strength to act on specific issues. In environments characterized by dynamism and constant change, coalitions, networks, and new alliances are likely to emerge. Efforts made to engage communities will affect the nature of public and private programs, policies, and resource allocation. Those implementing efforts to engage a community must be prepared to anticipate and respond to these changes.

> Community engagement will create changes in relationships and in the way institutions and individuals demonstrate their capacity and strength to act on specific issues.

9. Community collaboration requires long-term commitment by the engaging organization and its partners.

Communities and community collaborations differ in their stage of development (see the active community engagement continuum and diffusion of innovation in Chapter 1). As noted earlier, community engagement sometimes occurs around a specific, time-limited initiative. More commonly, however, community participation and mobilization need nurturing over the long term. Moreover, long-term partnerships have the greatest capacity for making a difference in the health of the population. Not surprisingly, building trust and helping communities develop the capacity and infrastructure for successful community action takes time. Before individuals and organizations can gain influence and become players and partners in decision making and action steps taken by communities relative to their health, they may need additional resources, knowledge, and skills. For example, partners might need long-term technical assistance and training related to developing an organization, securing resources, organizing constituencies to work for change, participating in partnerships and coalitions, resolving conflict, and other technical knowledge necessary to address issues of concern. Furthermore, strategies must be developed for sustaining efforts. The probability of sustained engagement and effective programming increases when community participants are active partners in the process.

CONCLUSION

In this chapter, we presented nine principles that are essential to the success of community-engaged health promotion and research. As noted in Chapter 1, however, community engagement is a continuum, and its specifics must be determined in response to the nature of one's endeavor and the organizational and community context in which it occurs. The next chapter will provide examples of how these principles have been applied in specific collaborative efforts.

3

Successful Examples in the Field

Chapter 3
Successful Examples in the Field

Robert Duffy, MPH (Chair), Sergio Aguilar-Gaxiola, MD, PhD, Donna Jo McCloskey, RN, PhD, Linda Ziegahn, PhD, Mina Silberberg, PhD

SUCCESSFUL EFFORTS IN COMMUNITY ENGAGEMENT

This chapter presents examples of successful community engagement efforts in health promotion, evaluation, and research that demonstrate the principles of engagement discussed in Chapters 1 and 2. The authors asked representatives from federal health agencies to recommend case examples of the effective use of community engagement that were published in peer-reviewed journals from 1997 to the present. Of the examples submitted, 12 are presented here. This chapter summarizes the articles associated with each case, emphasizing collaboration and the way the case illustrates the principles of interest. Information is up to date as of the time of the article's publication. At the end of each case, references and websites are provided for further information regarding findings, funding sources, and follow-up. The 12 examples are as follows:

1. Community Action for Child Health Equity (CACHÉ)
2. Health-e-AME

3. Project SuGAR
4. The Community Health Improvement Collaborative (CHIC)
5. Healing of the Canoe
6. Formando Nuestro Futuro/Shaping Our Future
7. Improving American Indian Cancer Surveillance and Data Reporting in Wisconsin
8. Children And Neighbors Defeat Obesity/La Comunidad Ayudando A Los Niños A Derrotar La Obesidad (CAN DO Houston)
9. The Dental Practice-Based Research Network
10. Diabetes Education & Prevention with a Lifestyle Intervention Offered at the YMCA (DEPLOY) Pilot Study
11. Project Dulce
12. Determinants of Brushing Young Children's Teeth

TABLE 3.1. MATRIX OF CASE EXAMPLES[1]

The following matrix summarizes the principles of community engagement illustrated by each of the case studies. The rationale for the selection of principles is included in each example.

Case Example	Principle 1 Be clear about the population/ communities to be engaged and the goals of the effort.	Principle 2 Know the community, including its norms, history, and experience with engagement efforts.	Principle 3 Build trust and relationships and get commitments from formal and informal leadership.	Principle 4 Collective self-determination is the responsibility and right of all community members.	Principle 5 Partnering with the community is necessary to create change and improve health.	Principle 6 Recognize and respect community cultures and other factors affecting diversity in designing and implementing approaches.	Principle 7 Sustainability results from mobilizing community assets and developing capacities and resources.	Principle 8 Be prepared to release control to the community and be flexible enough to meet its changing needs.	Principle 9 Community collaboration requires long-term commitment
1. CACHÉ	X	X	X	X	X	X		X	X
2. Health-e-AME	X	X	X	X	X				
3. Project SuGAR	X	X	X	X	X	X			X
4. CHIC		X	X		X		X	X	
5. Healing of the Canoe				X	X		X	X	X
6. Formando Nuestro Futuro/Shaping Our Future		X	X					X	X
7. Improving American Indian Cancer Surveillance and Data Reporting in Wisconsin		X	X		X	X			X
8. CAN DO Houston		X		X				X	
9. The Dental Practice-Based Research Network				X	X	X			
10. The DEPLOY Pilot Study			X	X	X		X		
11. Project Dulce					X	X	X		X
12. Determinants of Brushing Young Children's Teeth		X				X			

[1] The principles of community engagement have been abbreviated for this table.

1. COMMUNITY ACTION FOR CHILD HEALTH EQUITY (CACHÉ)

Background: In 2002, the National Institute of Child Health and Human Development (NICHD) began funding a five-site Community Child Health Network (CCHN) to examine how community, family, and individual factors interact with biological causes to result in health disparities in perinatal outcomes and in mortality and morbidity during infancy and early childhood. A large national cohort of families was recruited at the time of delivery with oversampling among African American and Latina women, women with preterm births, and low-income families. The investigators periodically assessed mothers and fathers, measuring individual, family, community, and institutional stressors as well as resilience factors. The three-phase study was designed to (1) develop academic-community partnerships and pilot studies; (2) conduct a longitudinal observational study to identify the pathways that lead to the disparities of interest, which would be informed by the initial developmental work; and (3) field a systematic study of sustainable interventions to eliminate these disparities, again informed by the observational study. At the time of publication, Phase 1 had been completed and Phase 2, also funded by NICHD, was under way.

CACHÉ is a partnership between the NorthShore Research Institute Section for Child and Family Health Studies and the Lake County Health Department/Community Health Center Women's Health Services. CACHÉ is a CCHN site in Lake County, located north of Chicago. During Phase 1, the county had 702,682 residents, comprising a diverse mix of individuals from varied races, ethnicities, and socioeconomic status. Even though Lake County had low unemployment between 2000 and 2005, 7.1% of the residents lived below the poverty line (Illinois Poverty Summit, 2005).

Methods: Community-based participatory research (CBPR) approaches were used for this study. Following a kickoff meeting, 27 community leaders volunteered to participate in a community advisory committee (CAC) that still shares in all program decision making. Interviews with these leaders were analyzed and findings shared with the CAC.

Results: This initial process allowed the community members to come to a consensus about the issues facing the Lake County families. The academic researchers and the community were able to create a vision for CACHÉ and a mission statement written in the language of the CAC. As CACHÉ transitioned from Phase 1 to Phase 2, the sustainability of the CAC was addressed through an open-door policy for CAC members. Each member was asked to bring whoever they thought was "missing at the table" for the next meeting.

At the national level, community advisors informed academics that collecting saliva or whole blood spots from men in the community would be viewed suspiciously because of a legacy of distrust in this population and concerns regarding confidentiality. In contrast, CACHÉ CAC members insisted that all clinically relevant testing be offered to fathers and mothers (with adequate explanation of the reasons for testing) and that clinical outreach and referral be offered in cases of abnormal findings. CACHÉ found additional foundation funding to pay for biospecimen collection from fathers, as well as a clinical tracking system and a part-time clinical social worker to provide triage and referrals.

One challenge to a long-term relationship between academic researchers and community organizations is the perception that the academic team has an unfair advantage in writing grants to obtain scarce funds from local foundations. CACHÉ attempts to overcome this challenge by offering technical assistance for preparing submissions for foundation grants to any agency that belongs to its collective.

Comments: Community wisdom brought to bear on the research process addressed local needs and moved CACHÉ to be highly innovative in both the collection of biospecimens from fathers and the communication of clinically relevant research findings to research participants in real time.

Applications of Principles of Community Engagement: The decisions and the decision-making roles that community members and academic members assumed during the initial development phase of CACHÉ exemplify many of the principles of community engagement. The decision to form a partnership with the community by creating a CAC was in line with Principles 1–5. The CAC shared in the process of creating a mission statement, and the collaboration continued throughout this long-term program (Principle 9). One unique aspect of CACHÉ is its insistence that goals be consistent with the overall CCHN objectives but be modified for local conditions. By including the collection of biospecimens against the advice of the CCHN but in response to the needs of Lake County, the CACHÉ program exemplifies Principle 6, which stresses that all aspects of community engagement must recognize and respect community diversity, and Principle 8, which cautions that an engaging organization must be prepared to release control of actions or interventions to the community and be flexible enough to meet the changing needs of that community. Finally, by responding constructively to perceptions that the academic team had an unfair advantage in writing grants, CACHÉ is using Principle 2, which acknowledges that the initiator of community engagement, in this case researchers, must become knowledgeable about the community's experience with engagement efforts and the community's perceptions of those initiating the engagement activities.

References

Illinois Poverty Summit. *2005 report on Illinois poverty.* 2005. Retrieved Mar 25, 2010, from http://www.heartlandalliance.org/maip.

Shalowitz M, Isacco A, Barquin N, Clark-Kauffman E, Delger P, Nelson D, et al. Community-based participatory research: a review of the literature with strategies for community engagement. *Journal of Developmental and Behavioral Pediatrics* 2009;30(4):350-361.

Websites

www.northshore.org/research/priorities

www.nichd.nih.gov/research/supported/cchn.cfm

2. HEALTH-E-AME

Background: The Medical University of South Carolina (MUSC) and the African Methodist Episcopal (AME) church had worked together on several health-related projects prior to this initiative. A needs assessment completed in 2002 with a sample of AME members revealed that physical activity (PA) was low. The AME Planning Committee, a group comprising AME members, pastors, and presiding elders as well as members of academic institutions, identified PA as an important target for reducing health disparities. MUSC, the University of South Carolina, and the AME Planning Committee then collaborated on a proposal to CDC. All three organizations participated actively in the proposal and the subsequent project, although the church opted to have the two universities handle the grant funds.

Methods: A CBPR approach using a randomized design with a delayed intervention control group.

The Health-e-AME Faith-Based PA Initiative was a three-year project funded through a CDC CBPR grant. Because a traditional randomized controlled design was not acceptable to AME church leaders, a randomized design with a delayed-intervention control group was chosen instead.

Results: More than 800 volunteers from 303 churches participated in the program. Among survey respondents as a whole, PA did not increase significantly over time. However, 67% of respondents were aware of the program, and program awareness was significantly related to PA outcomes and to consumption of fruits and vegetables. Pastoral support was significantly associated with increased PA.

Comments: The successful partnership between the researchers and the AME church continues to this day through the newly formed FAN (Faith, Activity, and Nutrition) initiative. Those wishing to participate in partnerships between academic and faith-based organizations can glean useful information from Health-e-AME, including the process partnerships can use to develop, implement, and evaluate PA interventions. PA interventions that actively engage faith-based organizations in decision making and program implementation are rare, making this approach and the lessons learned unique.

The successful partnership between the researchers and the AME church continues to this day through the newly formed FAN (Faith, Activity, and Nutrition) initiative.

Applications of Principles of Community Engagement: The researchers' partnership with the AME church reflects Principle 3, which asks organizers of community engagement to establish relationships and work with existing leadership structures. The initiative was designed to increase participation in PA among adult members of the AME church community. All decisions are based on active input and approval from the AME church. In this way, the project is built on Principle 4, which stresses that those engaging a community cannot assume that they know what is best for the community. Instead, decision making must occur on a partnership basis that results in shared power and mutual understanding. This group collaboration also reflects Principles 1–5 by establishing relationships and trust, allowing community control, and developing partnerships for change. MUSC, the University of South Carolina, and the AME Planning Committee have collaborated throughout, beginning with the CDC application for a CBPR grant. Because the partners have worked together from the beginning of the grant proposal and all decisions have been made through active input, this program exemplifies many of the principles of community engagement.

References

Wilcox S, Laken M, Anderson T, Bopp M, Bryant D, Carter R, et al. The health-e-AME faith-based physical activity initiative: description and baseline findings. *Health Promotion Practice* 2007;8(1):69-78.

Wilcox S, Laken M, Bopp M, Gethers O, Huang P, McClorin L, et al. Increasing physical activity among church members: community-based participatory research. *American Journal of Preventive Medicine* 2007;32(2):131-138.

3. PROJECT SUGAR

Background: Gullah-speaking African Americans have high rates of type 2 diabetes characterized by early onset and relatively high rates of complications (Sale et al., 2009). Researchers hoped to discover diabetes-specific alleles in this community because the Gullahs have a lower admixture of non-African genes in their genetic makeup than any other African American population in the United States due to their geographic isolation on the South Carolina coastline and islands. In addition to the scientific objective of identifying the genetics behind diabetes, Project SuGAR (Sea Island Genetic African American Family Registry) had an important second objective: to provide community outreach to promote health education and health screenings relative to metabolic and cardiovascular diseases.

Methods: The project used a CBPR approach. Investigators organized a local citizen advisory committee (CAC) to ensure that the research design was sensitive to the cultural and ethnic background of the community. This committee was involved in all phases of the research study.

Results: Services provided to the community included health education fairs, cultural fairs, a mobile "SuGAR Bus" to conduct health screenings, and jobs for community members who were staff on the project. Investigators exceeded their enrollment goal with 615 African American families, totaling 1,230 people, contributing to the genome study. The success of their recruitment strategy helped researchers create a world-class DNA registry that has been used to identify markers for diabetes, including novel type 2 diabetes loci for an African American population on chromosomes 14q and 7.

Comment: The success of the community engagement employed by Project SuGAR is further evidenced by the fact that the local CAC that started in 1996 is still operating today with the dual goals of establishing a family registry with DNA and developing long-term collaborations to promote preventative health. Under the new name Sea Islands Families Project, the local CAC oversees the use of the Project SuGAR registry and has branched out into similar community engagement projects such as Systemic Lupus Erythematosus in Gullah Health and South Carolina Center of

> The success of the community engagement employed by Project SuGAR is further evidenced by the fact that the local CAC that started in 1996 is still operating today with the dual goals of establishing a family registry with DNA and developing long-term collaborations to promote preventative health.

Biomedical Research Excellence for Oral Health. The local CAC adheres to the principles of CBPR and advocates community input at the initial development of the research plan. To this end, investigators who are new to the Gullah community and interested in community-based genetic research are asked to present their research plan to the council members before initiation of research projects. Investigators are also asked to present their findings as well as any publications to the group.

Applications of Principles of Community Engagement: Project SuGAR exemplifies Principles 1–6, which ask researchers to be clear about the purposes or goals of the engagement effort, learn about the community, and establish long-term goals based on community self-determination. Consistent with these principles, this partnership used a local CAC to ensure that the goals of the researchers were consistent with the goals of the community. The ongoing nature of the MUSC-Gullah collaboration illustrates Principle 9.

References

Fernandes JK, Wiegand RE, Salinas CF, Grossi SG, Sanders JJ, Lopes-Virella MF, et al. Periodontal disease status in Gullah African Americans with type 2 diabetes living in South Carolina. *Journal of Periodontology* 2009;80(7):1062-1068.

Johnson-Spruill I, Hammond P, Davis B, McGee Z, Louden D. Health of Gullah families in South Carolina with type 2 diabetes: diabetes self-management analysis from Project SuGar. *The Diabetes Educator* 2009;35(1):117-123.

Spruill I. Project Sugar: a recruitment model for successful African-American participation in health research. *Journal of National Black Nurses Association* 2004;15(2):48-53.

Sale MM, Lu L, Spruill IJ, Fernandes JK, Lok KH, Divers J, et al. Genome-wide linkage scan in Gullah-speaking African American families with type 2 diabetes: the Sea Islands Genetic African American Registry (Project SuGAR). *Diabetes* 2009;58(1):260-267.

Websites

http://academicdepartments.musc.edu/sugar/progress.htm

http://clinicaltrials.gov/ct2/show/NCT00756769

http://academicdepartments.musc.edu/cobre/overview.html

4. THE COMMUNITY HEALTH IMPROVEMENT COLLABORATIVE (CHIC): BUILDING AN ACADEMIC COMMUNITY PARTNERED NETWORK FOR CLINICAL SERVICES RESEARCH

Background: In 1992, CDC funded Healthy African American Families (HAAF) to study the reasons for high rates of low birth weight and infant mortality among African Americans in Los Angeles. The success of this collaboration led to the expansion of HAAF to investigate other health issues, including preterm delivery, mental health, diabetes, asthma, and kidney disease, as well as to look at various women's health projects. The academic component of HAAF evolved into the development of a research infrastructure, the Los Angeles Community Health Improvement Collaborative (CHIC). The purpose of CHIC was to encourage shared strategies, partnerships, and resources to support rigorous, community-engaged health services research within Los Angeles that was designed to reduce health disparities. Partners in the collaborative were the RAND Health Program; the University of California, Los Angeles (UCLA), branch of the Robert Wood Johnson Clinical Scholars Program at the David Geffen School of Medicine; the UCLA Family Medicine Research Center; three NIH centers (at UCLA, RAND, and Charles R. Drew University of Medicine and Science); the Los Angeles County Department of Health Services; the Los Angeles Unified School District; the Department of Veterans Affairs Greater Los Angeles Health Care System; Community Clinical Association of Los Angeles County; HAAF; and QueensCare Health and Faith Partnership.

> The success of this collaboration led to the expansion of HAAF to investigate other health issues, including preterm delivery, mental health, diabetes, asthma, and kidney disease, as well as to look at various women's health projects.

Methods: A CBPR approach using the principles of community engagement was employed to develop a community-academic council to coordinate the efforts of several research and training programs housed at three academic institutions.

Results: The conceptual framework developed for CHIC emphasizes the use of community engagement to integrate community and academic perspectives and develop programs that address the health priorities of communities while building the capacity of the partnership. Priorities for developing the research infrastructure included enhanced public participation in research, assessment of the community context, development of health information technology, and initiation of practical trial designs. Key challenges to addressing those priorities included (1) obtaining funding for community partners; (2) modifying evidence-based programs for underserved communities; (3) addressing diverse community priorities; (4) achieving the scale and obtaining the data needed for evaluation; (5) accommodating competing needs of community and academic partners; and (6) communicating effectively, given different expectations among partners.

Comments: With strong leadership and collaboration based on the principles of community engagement, it is feasible to develop an infrastructure that supports community engagement in clinical services research through collaboration across NIH centers and the sharing of responsibilities for infrastructure development, conceptual frameworks, and pilot studies.

Applications of Principles of Community Engagement: Interventions developed by CHIC are designed to meet research standards for effectiveness and community standards for validity and cultural sensitivity. The engagement process of first forming the partnership between the convening academic researchers and the community organizations and then deciding on health priorities together demonstrates Principle 5, and knowledge of community needs demonstrates Principle 2. Community participation demonstrates Principle 3, and the convener's flexibility in meeting the needs of the community demonstrates Principle 8. After four tracer conditions were established (depression, violence, diabetes, and obesity), the CHIC presented four areas for development of research capacity in line with several of the community engagement principles: public participation in all phases of research (Principle 5), understanding community and organizational context for clinical services interventions (Principles 2 and 3), practical methods for clinical services trials (Principle 8), and advancing health information technology for clinical services research (Principle 7).

References

Jones L, Wells K. Strategies for academic and clinician engagement in community-participatory partnered research. *JAMA* 2007;297(4):407-410.

Wells KB, Staunton A, Norris KC, Bluthenthal R, Chung B, Gelberg L, et al. Building an academic-community partnered network for clinical services research: the Community Health Improvement Collaborative (CHIC). *Ethnicity and Disease* 2006:16(1 Suppl 1):S3-17.

Website

http://haafii.org/HAAF_s_History.html

5. HEALING OF THE CANOE

Background: The Suquamish Tribe is a federally recognized tribe that resides on the Port Madison Indian Reservation in the rural Puget Sound area of Washington state. Of the tribe's more than 800 members, approximately 350 live on the reservation. The University of Washington's Alcohol and Drug Abuse Institute and the Suquamish Tribe have a partnership that began when the director of the tribe's Wellness Program inquired about the possibility of collaborating on the development of culturally relevant interventions on substance abuse in the community. At the same time, NIH's National Center on Minority Health and Health Disparities had called for three-year planning grants for CBPR with communities to address issues of health disparities. Following approval by the Tribal Council, an application was submitted and subsequently granted. The Healing of the Canoe (HOC) set out to reduce health disparities by (1) conducting assessments of community needs and resources; (2) identifying and prioritizing the health disparities of greatest concern to the community; (3) identifying strengths and resources already in the community that could be used to address concerns; (4) developing appropriate, community-based, and culturally relevant interventions; and (5) pilot testing the interventions.

Methods: The project used CBPR and tribal-based research approaches, the Community Readiness model (Pleasted et al., 2005), interviews with key stakeholders, and focus groups from four populations identified by the Suquamish Cultural Cooperative (SCC) and the researchers: Elders, youth, service providers, and other interested community members recruited through flyers, word of mouth, and personal recommendations.

Results: Key stakeholders and focus group participants identified several behavioral health issues of concern. Of particular concern were prevention of substance abuse among youth and the need for youth to have a sense of tribal identity and a sense of belonging to the community. Participants identified three strengths/resources in their community that they thought would be critical to addressing the areas of concern: the tribal Elders, tribal youth, and Suquamish culture and traditions.

Comments: The findings from this community assessment were used to develop a culturally grounded curriculum for Suquamish youth called "Holding Up Our Youth" that incorporated traditional values, practices, teachings, and stories to promote a sense of tribal identity and of belonging in the community. The result was an intervention that uses the canoe journey as a metaphor, providing youth with the skills needed to navigate through life without being pulled off course by alcohol or drugs, with culture and tradition serving as both anchor and compass (Pleasted et al., 2005; Thomas et al., 2010).

Applications of Principles of Community Engagement: The HOC project, by asking the community to identify its key health issues, demonstrates Principle 4, which states that communities need to "own" the issues, name the problems, identify action areas, plan and implement action strategies, and evaluate outcomes. Principle 7, which emphasizes the need to build on the capacity and assets of the community, is also evident in the project as it sought to identify the strengths and resources within the community. True partnership, as stressed in Principle 5, is evident at both the macro and micro levels in the HOC. A tribe member with a master's degree in social work is part of the research team and a coinvestigator. Following the completion of stakeholder interviews and focus groups, the HOC submitted a report to the SCC for review, feedback, suggestions, and approval, all in accordance with Principle 8, which states that principal investigators must be prepared to release control to the community. Finally, the foundation that was set by including the Suquamish Tribe in all aspects of the HOC project allowed for continued collaboration over time, in synchrony with Principle 9, long-term commitment by the engaging organization

References

Pleasted BA, Edwards RW, Jumper-Thurman P. *Community readiness: a handbook for successful change.* Fort Collins (CO): Tri-Ethnic Center for Prevention Research; 2005.

Thomas LR, Donovan DM, Sigo RLW. Identifying community needs and resources in a native community: a research partnership in the Pacific northwest. *International Journal of Mental Health and Addiction* 2010;8(2):362-373.

Websites

http://adai.washington.edu/canoe/history.htm

www.wcsap.org/Events/PDF/CR%20Handbook%20SS.pdf

6. FORMANDO NUESTRO FUTURO/SHAPING OUR FUTURE

Background: Formando Nuestro Futuro/Shaping Our Future (Formando) is a CBPR project focused on type 2 diabetes within the Hispanic farmworker communities in southeastern Idaho. In Idaho and elsewhere in the U.S., Hispanic farmworkers are at risk for many health conditions. This effort, which involved Idaho State University, evolved out of the Hispanic Health Project (HHP), a needs assessment survey conducted in 1998–1999, a review of diabetes charts at a community health center performed in 2000, and a binational ethnographic project conducted in 2001. Interestingly, there was a discrepancy between the community health clinic's estimate of the magnitude of the diabetes problem and the farmworkers' estimate.

Methods: The project used CBPR approaches that employed needs assessment and qualitative and quantitative methods. In 2001, to uncover the true effect of diabetes in the farmworker community, the HHP engaged in a binational ethnographic study of families that were split between Guanajuato, Mexico, and southeastern Idaho. A team of university researchers, promotores (community health workers), and students interviewed families in Guanajuato and southeastern Idaho.

Results: Some individuals described causes of diabetes that are congruent with the medical literature: herencia (heredity), mala nutrición (poor nutrition), and gordura (obesity). However, other individuals attributed their diabetes to such causes as susto (fright), coraje (anger), or preocupaciónes (worries). Thematic analysis of the interviews demonstrated that ideas about diabetes were linked to ideas of personal susceptibility; having diabetes was a stigmatized condition that connoted weakness. Individuals with diabetes were seen as weaker and vulnerable to being shocked and physically harmed by situations that others could withstand.

Comments: In 2004, Formando used the results from the ethnographic project to create a dialogue between the health care workers and the community of farmworkers. Currently, promotores visit each family once or twice a year to conduct interviews and collect data on biomarkers of diabetes. A series of educational modules is being presented at each home visit throughout the five-year study. These modules are based on the questions that the participants had during the previous round of visits from the

> Currently, promotores visit each family once or twice a year to conduct interviews and collect data on biomarkers of diabetes.

promotores. In this way, the educational component of the intervention builds continuously on the questions and previous lessons that the families have had. The long-term commitment to using the CBPR approach in these agricultural communities is an effective way to engage in health research and to establish real and meaningful dialogue with community members.

Applications of Principles of Community Engagement: Uncovering the hidden health problems of the Hispanic farmworker families requires researchers to use Principle 2, which emphasizes the need to become knowledgeable about the community's culture, economic conditions, and other factors. The HHP's success in working continuously with the community of southeastern Idaho farmers is evidence of its long-term commitment to community engagement (Principle 9) and to its ability to establish relationships and work with existing leadership (Principle 3). Finally, the process by which the Formando project evolved and the development of educational modules based on a specific family's questions about diabetes is illustrative of Principle 8, which stipulates that an engaging organization must be prepared to release control of interventions and be flexible enough to meet a community's changing needs.

Reference

Cartwright E, Schow D, Herrera S, Lora Y, Mendez M, Mitchell D, et al. Using participatory research to build an effective type 2 diabetes intervention: the process of advocacy among female Hispanic farmworkers and their families in Southeast Idaho. *Women and Health* 2006;43(4):89-109.

Website

www.isu.edu/~carteliz/publications.htm

7. IMPROVING AMERICAN INDIAN CANCER SURVEILLANCE AND DATA REPORTING IN WISCONSIN

Background: In 2002, Spirit of EAGLES, a Special Populations Network program funded by the National Cancer Institute to address comprehensive cancer control through partnerships with American Indian communities, and its partners submitted a letter of intent in response to an invitation by the Great Lakes Inter-Tribal Council. After the Wisconsin Tribal Health Directors' Association had reviewed the letter, Spirit of EAGLES and its partners were invited to prepare a full proposal for submission as part of the larger Great Lakes Native American Research Center for Health grant proposal to NIH and the Indian Health Service. Following scientific review, this cancer surveillance research study was funded and conducted through a subcontract to Spirit of EAGLES.

Initially, the project staff spent significant time traveling and meeting with the director and staff of each American Indian tribal and urban health clinic in the state. Eight of the 11 Wisconsin tribes and one urban health center agreed to partner in the project. These nine partners decided that Spirit of EAGLES and the academic staff of the University of Wisconsin Paul B. Carbone Comprehensive Cancer Center in Madison should be responsible for the coordination of this large, multisite project. The clinics agreed to participate in each step of the research study and to audit the cancer cases in their records. Funds were provided to each participating clinic to help offset the demands on their staff time. All partners agreed to a core set of questions to be answered by abstracting data from clinic records, but the clinics could include additional questions specific to their community.

Methods: The project had two phases: (1) a community-specific phase to provide each participating American Indian health clinic with a retrospective profile of its cancer burden, and (2) a statewide phase in which all the cases identified by the individual health clinics were matched with the state cancer registry and an aggregate report was prepared.

Project staff taught staff members at the American Indian clinics how to abstract data; after abstraction, the data were analyzed at the Great Lakes Tribal Epidemiology Center. Spirit of EAGLES and staff at the center drafted an individual report for each community that described its cancer burden. American Indian health directors, clinic staff, and project staff met to discuss and interpret findings. Final, clinic-specific reports were presented to each clic. Presentations were made to health boards or tribal government committees as requested.

During the second phase, staff from the Wisconsin Cancer Reporting System matched cancer cases to the state registry and provided a de-identified database to tribal epidemiology center staff, who analyzed the aggregate data. At the time of publication, a draft report of the aggregate data and matches had been developed and presented for review and input at a meeting of the Wisconsin Tribal Health Directors' Association. The final aggregate report was to be disseminated to each participating community; each community would receive a report of the match between the cancer cases identified by its clinic and those identified by the Wisconsin Cancer Reporting System.

Results: Assessing the local cancer burden of American Indian communities in Wisconsin and improving the accuracy of the state American Indian cancer data necessitated multisite partnerships. Project leads embraced and used the diversity of backgrounds, skills, and experience of the partnering institutions.

> This project demonstrates the successful application of CBPR in a complex, multisite project with multiple partners.

Comments: This project demonstrates the successful application of CBPR in a complex, multisite project with multiple partners. The approach developed reflected the time, availability, and skills of all partners; it was acceptable to all those involved and not unduly burdensome to any one individual or group. The project's success is measured not only in terms of improving the accuracy of cancer data for American Indians in Wisconsin but also by the ongoing, deeper relationships that were formed. At the time of publication, an independent evaluation of the project was being conducted, and new collaborations were under way.

Applications of Principles of Community Engagement: This project, a CBPR effort among diverse partners, adheres to Principle 3, which asks organizers of community engagement to establish relationships and work with existing structures. Working with multiple sites through several organizations within a community allows organizers to form a true partnership, as stressed by Principle 5. By using CBPR, the project acknowledges Principle 2, which stresses the importance of understanding the community's perceptions of those initiating the engagement activities. This is of utmost importance because of the history of racism suffered by American Indian communities and the mistreatment of some American Indians by researchers, which has fostered mistrust of researchers. The researchers also circumvented mistrust by putting extra emphasis on ways to deepen trust between partners. One example was the researchers' return of raw data to the health directors and clinic staff for interpretation; this allowed the clinic personnel to give unique perspectives on the data, and some community-specific cancer interventions were developed using their insights. In addition, by sharing the data with all the different clinics, the project reflected the clinics' diversity, as stressed in Principle 6. Finally, through its four years of partnership and the potential for more projects in the future, this program demonstrates Principle 9, which states that long-term commitment is required for community engagement to truly succeed.

Reference

Matloub J, Creswell PD, Strickland R, Pierce K, Stephenson L, Waukau J, et al. Lessons learned from a community-based participatory research project to improve American Indian cancer surveillance. *Progress in Community Health Partnerships: Research, Education, and Action* 2009;3(1):47-52.

Websites

www.cancer.wisc.edu/uwccc/outreach.asp

http://mayoresearch.mayo.edu/cancercenter/spirit_of_eagles.cfm

8. CHILDREN AND NEIGHBORS DEFEAT OBESITY/LA COMUNIDAD AYUDANDO A LOS NIÑOS A DERROTAR LA OBESIDAD (CAN DO HOUSTON)

Background: After *Men's Fitness* magazine named Houston the "Fattest City in America" in 2005, the Office of the Mayor initiated the Mayor's Wellness Council (MWC) to encourage and motivate Houstonians to eat healthfully and engage in regular physical activity. The following year, the MWC created the Houston Wellness Association (HWA), a nonprofit association that endeavored to engage businesses and the wellness industry in efforts to increase the wellness of all Houston residents. Through informal networks of HWA and MWC members, momentum and interest began to grow, and a large consortium of stakeholders, including city services, experts in health disparities and childhood obesity, pediatricians, universities, and community programs, coordinated efforts to tackle childhood obesity. From this collaboration, CAN DO Houston (Children And Neighbors Defeat Obesity; la Comunidad Ayudando a los Niños a Derrotar la Obesidad) was created as a comprehensive, community-based childhood obesity prevention program.

Methods: CAN DO Houston stakeholders chose the city's Sunnyside and Magnolia Park neighborhoods to be the pilot sites for the program. They then selected an elementary school and park within each neighborhood to serve as anchors for the program. With the locations finalized, the stakeholders researched the available programs in the Houston area that addressed childhood obesity. They posted a database of more than 60 programs online so the participants in the program could become aware of and use them. Subsequently, interviews were conducted with key informants, including the school principals, park managers, physical education teachers, staff of the Metropolitan Transit Authority of Harris County, and police officers, to prioritize the needs for each community. Additionally, CAN DO Houston held multiple focus groups with parents from Sunnyside and Magnolia Park. Interviewees and the focus group members were asked to describe both strengths and barriers in their communities relative to being physically active, accessing good nutrition, and developing healthy minds. They also were asked to identify and prioritize possible initiatives.

Results: The findings showed the unique strengths within each community as well as the specific challenges that the program initiatives could address. For example, in Magnolia Park, participants indicated that children had good access to resources for healthy eating, and in Sunnyside the participants indicated that children were engaging in more than the recommended 60 minutes of moderate-to-vigorous activity each day. The primary barrier identified in Magnolia Park was the lack of physical activity; in Sunnyside, it was the lack of education on nutrition for the children and parents. With this information, the CAN DO Houston program was able to tailor specific interventions for each community.

The interviews and focus groups in Magnolia Park revealed a safety and logistical problem that was contributing to the underuse of the free after-school program in the city park. The park was only 0.4 miles from the elementary school, but a busy four-lane street and a bayou prevented most parents from allowing their children to walk to it. To address the problem of safe access, CAN DO Houston partnered with the park recreation staff and arranged for them to conduct an after-school program at the school twice per week. The park staff led the activities, and CAN DO Houston provided volunteers to assist the park staff and supervise the students. More than 80 students signed up for the program. Because of the pilot's success, the school district agreed to provide bus transportation between the school and the park during the 2009–2010 school year.

> Because of the pilot's success, the school district agreed to provide bus transportation between the school and the park during the 2009–2010 school year.

In Sunnyside, CAN DO Houston coordinated a monthly wellness seminar to educate parents on good nutrition and various wellness topics. In addition, it offered tours of grocery stores that focused on how to buy healthy foods on a budget. A nutrition carnival was hosted during the park's after-school program, and the project provided the park with supplies to incorporate education on nutrition into this program.

Comment: The pilot initiative of CAN DO Houston successfully formed a consortium of people and organizations interested in addressing childhood obesity that continues to link Houston neighborhoods with resources that can be used to address the unique challenges that these communities face. CAN DO demonstrates that, through the use of existing resources, implementing a successful initiative on the prevention of childhood obesity in an urban setting is feasible even with minimal funding.

Applications of Principles of Community Engagement: More than 70 organizations participated in the development of the CAN DO Houston pilot program, establishing a broad collaboration of community members, institutions, organizations, and local government. Uniting so many groups reflects Principle 2, which asks organizers of community engagement to establish relationships and work with existing leadership structures. The implementers of CAN DO Houston coordinated various activities to promote healthy living, including after-school programs, grocery store tours, wellness seminars, cooking classes, and staff wellness clubs, all on the basis of the input and priorities of community members. By implementing the initiatives chosen by the community through the existing community organizations and resources, CAN DO Houston provides opportunities for partner ownership, consistent with Principle 4, which stresses that no external entity should assume that it can bestow on a community the power to act in its own self-interest. Finally, engaging and listening to the communities and allowing them to prioritize the initiatives of the program fulfills Principle 8, which counsels the engaging organization to be prepared to relinquish control of actions to the community.

Reference

Correa NP, Murray NG, Mei CA, Baun WB, Gor BJ, Hare NB, et al. CAN DO Houston: a community-based approach to preventing childhood obesity. *Preventing Chronic Disease* 2010;7(4):A88.

Website

http://ccts.uth.tmc.edu/ccts-services/can-do-houston

9. THE DENTAL PRACTICE-BASED RESEARCH NETWORK

Background: Practice-based research networks (PBRNs) are consortia of practices committed to improving clinical practice. Operating internationally since 2005, the Dental Practice-Based Research Network (DPBRN) is a collaborative effort of Kaiser Permanente Northwest/Permanente Dental Associates in Portland, Oregon; Health Partners of Minneapolis, Minnesota; University of Alabama at Birmingham; University of Copenhagen; Alabama Dental Practice Research Network; and clinicians and patients in Oregon, Washington, Minnesota, Florida, Alabama, Georgia, Mississippi, Norway, Sweden, and Denmark.

Methods: DPBRN began by obtaining patient input during feasibility/pilot testing of certain studies, then progressed to a study that formally included patient perceptions, and later made plans for a community advisory board. Additionally, patient representatives serve on an advisory committee managed by the main funder of DPBRN activities, the National Institute of Dental and Craniofacial Research.

Results: As different parties became familiar with each other's priorities, they were able to establish common ground and carry out successful collaborations. DPBRN has provided a context in which researchers and community clinicians collaborate as equals, and in keeping with the basic principles of CBPR, it engages patients as well. DPBRN practitioner-investigators and their patients have contributed to research at each stage of its development, leading to improvements in study designs and customization of protocols to fit daily clinical practice. At the time of publication, 19 studies had been completed or were ongoing. The studies include a broad range of topic areas, enrollments, and study designs.

Comments: DPBRN practitioners and patients from diverse settings are partnering with academic clinical scientists to improve daily clinical practice and meet the needs of clinicians and their patients. PBRNs can improve clinical practice by engaging in studies that are of direct interest to clinicians and their patients and by incorporating findings from these studies into practice. Patients' acceptance of these studies has been very high.

Applications of Principles of Community Engagement: The DPBRN exemplifies several principles of community engagement. For example, community practitioners are coming together with academicians to develop and answer relevant research questions that can directly affect daily clinical practice. By engaging dentists in private practice, the network is able to reach the site of dental care for concentrated groups of patients and to conduct research that spans the geographic, cultural, social, and rural/urban diversity of different patient populations. This ability to connect with different groups is congruent with the diversity required by Principle 6. Researchers are partnering with the DPBRN in a way that allows for practitioners in the community, who traditionally are outside of academic institutions, to participate in all stages of research (Principle 5). This can not only close the gap between academic and community practices but also empower the dentists to name the research questions and participate in the quest for solutions. This acknowledges Principle 4, which reminds researchers that no external entity can bestow on a community the power to act in its own self-interest.

References

Gilbert GH, Williams OD, Rindal DB, Pihlstrom DJ, Benjamin PL, Wallace MC. The creation and development of the dental practice-based research network. *Journal of the American Dental Association* 2008;139(1):74-81.

Makhija S, Gilbert GH, Rindal DB, Benjamin PL, Richman JS, Pihlstrom DJ. Dentists in practice-based research networks have much in common with dentists at large: evidence from the Dental Practice-Based Research Network. *General Dentistry* 2009;57(3):270-275.

10. DIABETES EDUCATION & PREVENTION WITH A LIFESTYLE INTERVENTION OFFERED AT THE YMCA (DEPLOY) PILOT STUDY

Background: With its exceptional reach into diverse U.S. communities and long history of implementing successful health promotion programs, the YMCA is a capable community partner. Over a period of four years, the YMCA of Greater Indianapolis participated with researchers at Indiana University School of Medicine (IUSM) to design, implement, and evaluate a group-based adaptation of the highly successful Diabetes Prevention Program (DPP) lifestyle intervention. This project, DEPLOY, was conducted to test the hypotheses that wellness instructors at the YMCA could be trained to implement a group-based lifestyle intervention with fidelity to the DPP model and that adults at high risk for developing diabetes who received this intervention could achieve changes in body weight comparable to those achieved in the DPP.

Methods: DEPLOY, a matched-pair, group-randomized pilot comparative effectiveness trial involving two YMCA facilities in greater Indianapolis, compared the delivery of a group-based DPP lifestyle intervention by the YMCA with brief counseling alone (control). The YMCA, which was engaged before the development of the research grant proposal, collaborated with researchers at IUSM throughout the study. Research participants were adults who attended a diabetes risk-screening event at one of two semi-urban YMCA facilities and had a BMI (kg/m²) greater than 24, two or more risk factors for diabetes, and a random capillary blood glucose concentration of 110–199 mg/dL. Multivariate regression was used to compare between-group differences in changes in body weight, blood pressures, hemoglobin A1c (glycosylated hemoglobin), total cholesterol, and HDL (high-density lipoprotein) cholesterol after six and 12 months.

Results: Among 92 participants after six months, body weight decreased by 6.0% in intervention participants and 2.0% in controls. Intervention participants also had greater changes in total cholesterol. These significant differences were sustained after 12 months, and adjustment for differences in race and sex did not alter the findings.

> Among 92 participants after six months, body weight decreased by 6.0% in intervention participants and 2.0% in controls.

Comments: With more than 2,500 facilities nationwide, the YMCA is a promising channel for wide-scale dissemination of a low-cost model for preventing diabetes by changing lifestyles.

Applications of Principles of Community Engagement: Bringing health promotion activities to members of the community often requires mobilizing the community's existing assets, both people and institutional resources, as described in Principle 7. In line with Principles 3, 4, 5, and 7, the YMCA was engaged before the development of the research grant proposal, and it collaborated on the study design, approach to recruiting, delivery of the intervention, development of measures, interpretation of results, and dissemination of findings. DEPLOY demonstrates how intensive programs designed to change lifestyles can be more sustainable when health care centers engage established social institutions like the YMCA.

Reference

Ackermann RT, Finch EA, Brizendine E, Zhou H, Marrero DG. Translating the Diabetes Prevention Program into the community. The DEPLOY pilot study. *American Journal of Preventive Medicine* 2008;35(4):357-363.

11. PROJECT DULCE

Background: Diabetes management programs have been found to improve health outcomes, and thus there is a need to translate and adapt them to meet the needs of minority, underserved, and underinsured populations. In 1997, a broad coalition of San Diego County health care and community-based organizations developed Project Dulce (Spanish for "sweet") to test the effectiveness of a community-based, culturally sensitive approach involving case management by nurses and peer education to improve diabetes care and elevate health status among a primarily Latino underserved community in Southern California. Partners included the San Diego Medically Indigent Adult program and San Diego County Medical Services.

Methods: The goals of the project are to meet the American Diabetes Association's standards of care and to achieve improvements in HbA1c (glycosylated hemoglobin), blood pressure, and lipid parameters. A bilingual team, consisting of a registered nurse/certified diabetes educator, a medical assistant, and a dietitian, travels to community clinics to see patients up to eight times per year, then enters patient-specific data into a computer registry that generates quarterly reports to guide future care. In addition to having one-on-one clinic visits with the Dulce team, patients are encouraged to participate in weekly peer education sessions.

At each clinic, "natural leaders" are identified out of the patient population with diabetes and trained to be peer educators or *promotores*. The training consists of a four-month competency-based and mentoring program that culminates with the promotor providing instruction in concert with an experienced educator.

The instructors use a detailed curriculum in teaching the weekly sessions in the patients' native language. The classes are collaborative, including interactive sessions in which the patients discuss their personal experiences and beliefs. Emphasis is placed on overcoming cultural factors, such as fear of using insulin, that are not congruent with self-management.

Results: Project Dulce's first group showed significant improvement in HbA1c, total cholesterol, and LDL (low-density lipoprotein) cholesterol compared with chart reviews of patients having similar demographics from the same

The success of the initial program has led to the creation of modified offshoots to address the diabetes-related needs of African American, Filipino, and Vietnamese communities.

clinics over the same time period. Participants' belief that personal control over their health was possible and that contact with medical service providers was important in maintaining health increased. The success of the initial program has led to the creation of modified offshoots to address the diabetes-related needs of African American, Filipino, and Vietnamese communities. In 2008, Project Dulce added the care management program of IMPACT (Improving Mood-Promoting Access to Collaborative Treatment) to address the problem of depression among patients at three community clinics serving a low-income, predominantly Spanish-speaking Latino population. Up to 33% of patients tested positive for symptoms of major depression upon entering the program, and intervention resulted in a significant decline in the depression identification scores.

Comments: The ability to adapt Project Dulce to new communities and new components attests to its potential as a vehicle to administer care to underserved populations.

Applications of Principles of Community Engagement: Project Dulce has been shown to help patients overcome many cultural barriers to care that can result in poor adherence to medical advice. A key to the program is the identification and training of individuals within the community to lead the intervention's interactive educational component. By facilitating the transformation of patients into peer educators, Project Dulce mobilizes the community's existing assets and incorporates Principle 7, which stresses capacity building for achieving community health goals. Creating a peer education group coupled with a bilingual/bicultural nursing team illustrates the true partnership prescribed by Principle 5, and it is a model for community engagement that can be modified appropriately to reflect cultural diversity, as stressed in Principle 6. After initial success within the Latino community, Project Dulce has been able to adapt its curriculum and group education approach to address the needs of other communities. At the time of publication, it had programs in eight languages. These adaptations respond to the diversity of San Diego County and are congruent with Principle 9, which emphasizes that a long-term commitment is required to improve community health outcomes.

References

Gilmer TP, Philis-Tsimikas A, Walker C. Outcomes of Project Dulce: a culturally specific diabetes management program. *Annals of Pharmacotherapy* 2005;39(5):817-822.

Gilmer TP, Roze S, Valentine WJ, Emy-Albrecht K, Ray JA, Cobden D, et al. Cost-effectiveness of diabetes case management for low-income populations. *Health Services Research* 2007;42(5):1943-1959.

Philis-Tsimikas A, Walker C, Rivard L, Talavera G, Reimann JO, Salmon M, et al. Improvement in diabetes care of underinsured patients enrolled in Project Dulce: a community-based, culturally appropriate, nurse case management and peer education diabetes care model. *Diabetes Care* 2004;27(1):110-115.

Website

http://www.scripps.org/services/diabetes/project-dulce

12. DETERMINANTS OF BRUSHING YOUNG CHILDREN'S TEETH: IMPLICATIONS FOR ANTICIPATORY BRUSHING GUIDANCE

Background: The roles played by health beliefs and norms, standards, and perceived self-efficacy have been largely untapped in studies of tooth-brushing behavior. Rural parents with limited incomes are more likely to be young and geographically isolated than their urban counterparts, and thus these rural parents might be less knowledgeable about where to turn for advice about oral health or to obtain oral health services. Moreover, even if parents are aware of and have access to resources for their children, rural parents might avoid using them, preferring to "get by" on their own or with the help of family members. Utilization data show that, overall, rural children are less likely than children living in other areas to use dental services overall and that rural parents are more likely to report the purpose of the last dental visit as something "bothering or hurting" their children.

Methods: Researchers from the University of Washington included parents and community-based health professionals in each step of the study design and data collection. Parents were interviewed as expert informants to elucidate a diverse set of viewpoints regarding the value and ease of brushing young children's teeth. Study protocols and the interview guide were reviewed, revised, and approved by a steering committee consisting of seven community residents, including five professionals in early childhood health or education and two low-income mothers with young children. Interviews were conducted by three paid community residents trained by the study investigators.

Results: Just under two-thirds (26 of 41) of the parents who reported the age at which they began brushing their child's teeth said it was before the child's first birthday. No single explanation emerged as a majority reason for initiating brushing. The most common reason was an external cue, such as the eruption of the child's first tooth. Other common reasons reflected health beliefs, followed by normative expectations, including advice from early childhood educators, health professionals, or peers.

Nearly all parents (91%) thought the recommendation to brush a child's teeth twice a day was realistic. However, only slightly more than half (55%) reported achieving this goal. Parents who achieved twice-daily brushing were more likely than those who did not achieve this standard to accurately discuss milestones in child development, children's oral health needs, and specific skills to engage the child's cooperation. The most common barriers to brushing, cited by 89% of all parents, were lack of time and an uncooperative child.

In summary, the study found that determinants of parents brushing their children's teeth vary. For this reason, rural children would benefit from simple interventions to encourage an early and regular habit of tooth brushing by their parents. Guidance given to parents about the oral health of their children should include discussion of ways to overcome the challenges identified in the study.

Comments: Because parents participated in the advisory board as expert informants on tooth brushing and served as study designers, data collectors, and study participants, new knowledge was generated.

Applications of Principles of Community Engagement: Principle 6 emphasizes that all aspects of community engagement must recognize and respect community diversity; this research project demonstrates this principle by acknowledging that the determinants of brushing the teeth of one's children vary. By going into the community and learning about the community's norms and values, the researchers were also demonstrating Principle 2.

Reference

Huebner CE, Riedy CA. Behavioral determinants of brushing young children's teeth: implications for anticipatory guidance. *Pediatric Dentistry* 2010;32(1):48-55.

CONCLUSION

This chapter provided examples of successful community engagement projects that took place in a variety of communities, including academic health centers, community-based organizations, churches, and the public health sector. Only 12 projects were presented here, but the literature now offers many such examples. However, little has been written about the organizational capacities required to make these efforts successful. The next chapter addresses the organizational supports necessary for effective community engagement.

Managing Organizational Support
for Community Engagement

Chapter 4
Managing Organizational Support for Community Engagement

Michael Hatcher, DrPH, David Warner, MD, Mark Hornbrook, MD

INTRODUCTION

A great deal has been researched and written on collaborative processes that support community engagement, but the literature does not offer a systematic review of how successful organizations provide the structural support needed to plan, initiate, evaluate, and sustain collaborative processes that produce collective community actions. Butterfoss (2007) states that a convening organization "must have sufficient organizational capacity, commitment, leadership, and vision to build an effective coalition" (p. 254). However, there is little research concerning these characteristics.

This chapter presents a review of frameworks to help organizations determine the capacity they need to support community engagement. It includes a set of testable propositions about required capacity. The frameworks have been developed by matching the structural capacities required for any endeavor as defined by Handler et al. (2001) with the prerequisites for effective community engagement identified through: (1) the nine principles of community engagement (Chapter 2), (2) community coalition action theory (CCAT; Butterfoss et al., 2009), and (3) the constituency development framework (Hatcher et al., 2001; Hatcher et al., 2008; Nicola et al., 2000).

THE FRAMEWORKS

Principles of Community Engagement

This document, like the first edition of *Principles of Community Engagement*, provides nine guiding principles for organizations to apply when working with community partners. These principles give organizational leaders a framework for shaping their own culture, planning engagement, conducting outreach, and interacting with communities. However, principles by themselves do not offer an engagement model or process for their application. The principles are certainly compatible with existing community mobilization processes, such as those outlined by the National Association of County and City Health Officials in *Mobilizing for Action through Partnership and Planning* (2011), but compatibility per se is not enough. To date, there has been no clear guidance on how to organizationally or operationally support the use of these nine principles or the array of community mobilization models.

Community Coalition Action Theory

As noted in Chapter 1, Butterfoss et al. (2009) articulated CCAT on the basis of research on the collaborative engagements of coalitions. In laying out CCAT, they provided 21 practice-based propositions that address processes ranging from the formation of coalitions through institutionalization. Like the principles of community engagement, however, CCAT does not identify the structural capacity and management support required to facilitate and guide the processes it recommends.

Among the frameworks used in the synthesis offered in this chapter, CCAT occupies a unique and important role because it ties community engagement to theory. In fact, it is a particularly appropriate theoretical framework because the CCAT developers are specifically interested in what Butterfoss (2007) describes as "formal, multipurpose, and long-term alliances" (p. 42), which are distinct from the activities of short-term coalitions that coalesce to address a single issue of concern and disband after it is resolved. Although CCAT is designed primarily to understand community coalitions, community engagement is not limited to coalition processes. Even so, CCAT and community engagement have a common focus on long-term relationships, and CCAT offers propositions that are clearly relevant for undertaking and sustaining collaborative processes for community engagement. Additionally, CCAT addresses the full range of processes from initiation of new collaborative activities to institutionalization of mature relationships. Finally, CCAT propositions support the nine principles of community engagement.

Constituency Development

The third framework described here is drawn from the organizational practice of constituency development; that is, the process of developing relationships with community members who benefit from or have influence over community public health actions. Constituency development involves four practice elements (Hatcher et al., 2008):

- Know the community, its constituents, and its capabilities.

- Establish positions and strategies that guide interactions with constituents.

- Build and sustain formal and informal networks to maintain relationships, communicate messages, and leverage resources.

- Mobilize communities and constituencies for decision making and social action.

This framework provides a parsimonious set of tasks that must be undertaken for community engagement. The question we seek to answer is how these tasks can be carried out in accordance with the principles of community engagement and CCAT. To specify the capacity required to support this effort, we use the categories of structural capacity delineated by Handler and colleagues (Handler et al., 2001), which include five kinds of resources: human, informational, organizational, physical, and fiscal. In *Public Health: What It Is and How It Works,* Turnock elaborates on these capacities as they apply to health systems (2009):

- Human resources include competencies such as leadership, management, community health, intervention design, and disciplinary sciences.

- Information resources span data and scientific knowledge, including demographic and socioeconomic data, data on health risks and health status, behavioral data, data on infrastructure and services, and knowledge-based information like that found in the intervention and disciplinary sciences that is used to guide health and community actions.

- Organizational resources include organizational units and missions; administrative, management, and service-delivery structures; coordinating structures; communication channels and networks; regulatory or policy guidance; and organizational and professional practices and processes.

- Physical resources are the work spaces and places, hardware, supplies, materials, and tools used to conduct business.

- Fiscal resources include the money used to perform within an enterprise area like health as well as the real and perceived economic values accumulated from the outputs of an enterprise. Fiscal resources are seldom discussed in literature regarding the health and community engagement enterprise within the public sector. The investment of money and time to engage communities in public sector processes, however, has many potential returns, including leveraging of the resources of partners, development of community services that may accrue income for reinvestment, synergistic actions that achieve the objectives of an enterprise, increases in social capital, and population health improvements that have economic value. As with all investments, those who commit to long-term and sustained community engagement most often accrue the greatest returns.

EXAMINING THE STRUCTURAL CAPACITY NEEDED FOR COMMUNITY ENGAGEMENT

Synthesizing the frameworks described above allows us to identify the structural capacity needs of organizations or agencies, coalitions, or other collaborative entities that are undertaking community engagement. Synthesis starts with the four practice elements of constituency development developed by Hatcher et al. (2008). Appendix 4.1 contains a table for each of the four practice elements (know the community, establish strategies, build networks, and mobilize communities) that sets forth its components in detail. The text here touches only on their major points.

Practice Element 1: Know the Community

The first practice element is focused on knowing the community's history and experience, its constituents, and their capabilities. In a sense, this practice element addresses the intelligence-gathering function behind planning, decision making, and leveraging resources to collaboratively achieve anticipated or agreed-upon outcomes with community partners. As depicted in Table 4.1, this element speaks to the need for a wide range of data types, secure reporting and collection systems, human skills and equipment to analyze and interpret data, organizational processes to communicate this information and foster its use in decision making, and a culture that values community-engaged information gathering and use. The goal is to enable all partners to understand diverse viewpoints on community issues and to appreciate the range of solutions that may address those issues.

The individuals and groups from communities or organizations undertaking engagement activities have differing abilities to assimilate data through their respective filters. If understanding is not developed collectively, it is often difficult to move to a collective decision or action. All but the smallest homogenous communities have multiple layers of complexity that require organized, collective ways to obtain and understand community information. In brief, understanding is rooted in experience, social and cultural perspectives, perceptions of influence, and the ability to act collaboratively within the engaging organization and the engaged community. Thus, the task of knowing a community must be approached as an organizational function and supported with sufficient capacity to collectively undertake this work.

> If understanding is not developed collectively, it is often difficult to move to a collective decision or action.

Practice Element 2: Establish Positions and Strategies

To successfully address Practice Element 2, structural capacity must be in place to identify the engaging organization's priorities regarding community health issues as well as any limitations in the organization's mission, funding, or politics that will restrain its ability to address those issues. The development of positions and strategies allows an organization to effectively plan its role in the community engagement process. In particular, it is critical to be clear about the organization's intentions and its ability to adjust and align its position to differing viewpoints and priorities likely to exist within the community. An introspective review will examine whether the organization is willing to adjust its priorities in response to the concerns of the community (i.e., takes an open position) or whether it insists on following its own internal priorities (a closed position). The answer to this question should drive the engagement strategy, and the organization must clearly communicate the degree to which it is open to change so that the community can have clear expectations about what can be collaboratively addressed.

Structural capacity is also needed to support the examination of external forces. The understanding of these forces, like the understanding of internal forces, is critical for establishing positions and strategies that facilitate social mobilization and participatory decision making. Another term for the examination of external forces would be "external planning." In particular, it is necessary to determine whether the community is capable of participating and whether it is ready to take action. If the community lacks capacity, it will be necessary to facilitate the development of its capacity. If the community has capacity but is not ready to act, strategies will need to be developed to help the community better understand the issues and create opportunities for it to act.

When establishing positions through internal and external planning, engagement leaders must consider multiple variables that influence health, including social, cultural, epidemiologic, behavioral, environmental, political, and other factors. An assessment of these factors will provide insight not only into possible targets for health actions but also into competing interests of the community and its potential responses to the organization's positions and strategies. Organizational positions should be developed through robust analyses and present the organization's views on the health issue, the range of possible solutions to that issue, and the rationale for engaging in collaborative action. The organization's strategy for gaining community support should underlie the method of presenting its position; the presentation should be designed to stimulate community dialogue and result in a determination of the community's expectations and the resulting collective position.

It is important to engage the community in this process as early as possible, although timing depends on the community's readiness. Regardless of the situation, the organization's capacity to analyze, establish, present, and manage positions and strategies will either facilitate or hinder the engagement process.

Building and maintaining the structural capacity to perform this work requires rigorous attention from engagement leaders. Specific insights into each capacity component for this practice element are presented in Table 4.2, which demonstrates that the structural capacity needs for this practice element are closely aligned with those of Practice Element 1.

Practice Element 3: Building and Sustaining Networks

Developing networks of collaborators is the third element in the organizational practice of community engagement. As described by Nicola and Hatcher, "developing networks is focused on establishing and maintaining relationships, communication channels, and exchange systems that promote linkages, alliances, and opportunities to leverage resources among constituent groups" (Nicola et al., 2000). In organizational practice, the development and maintenance of networks is a critical function and contributes to many organizational practice areas, specifically practices related to most of the 10 essential public health services identified by CDC 17 years ago (CDC, 1994). Effective community engagement networks should have active communication channels, fluid exchange of resources, and energetic coordination of collaborative activities among network partners. These targets can be achieved when organizations understand, support, and use available network structures. Keys to success include having the structural capacity to:

- Identify and analyze network structures (communication, power, and resource flow);

- Affiliate with those in existing networks;

- Develop and deliver ongoing messages across formal and informal communication channels to maintain information flow and coordinated activity;

- Target communications and resources to leverage agenda-setting processes within a community (Kozel et al., 2003; Kozel et al., 2006a, 2006b); and

- Establish, use, and monitor resource exchange systems that support network interactions and coordinated, collaborative community work.

Organizational leaders and managers must provide ongoing attention to building and maintaining the structural capacity to perform this work. The key task areas just described are dealt with more specifically in Table 4.3. The essential structural capacity needed for this practice element includes the skills and systems to communicate and relate to people on a personal basis, knowledge and understanding of community power structures, and access to communication and resource exchange networks.

Practice Element 4: Mobilizing Constituencies

The fourth and final practice element in community engagement is mobilizing constituencies, other organizations, or community members. Mobilization includes moving communities through the process of dialogue, debate, and decision making to obtain their commitment to a collaborative goal; determining who will do what and how it will be done; implementing activities; and monitoring, evaluating, adjusting, and reevaluating these activities in a cyclical fashion. Engagement leaders must be fully immersed in the building and maintaining of the structural capacity to perform this work. A key to this practice element is earning the trust required for obtaining community commitment. To this end, the engagement process must be honest, and expectations must be clear. Leaders in both the community and the engaging organization must be committed to meaningful negotiations to resolve any salient issues. Engagement efforts will flounder in the absence of transparency and reciprocity in the engagement process. Insights on the wide range of human skills, data, management structures, and material resources needed to support this practice element are found in Table 4.4.

...the engagement process must be honest, and expectations must be clear.

CONCLUSION

Effective community engagement requires a significant commitment to developing and mobilizing the organizational resources necessary to support engagement activities. This chapter has attempted a practical synthesis of how these frameworks identify the capacity needs of an engaging organization, but more work is needed to further develop and validate these capacities and their linkages between the propositions of CCAT, community engagement principles, and the organizational practice elements presented here. Among other considerations, such work should account for the considerable diversity that exists among organizations. Regardless, it is hoped that these practice-based observations and insights will be tested and refined and will ultimately lead to a greater understanding of how organizations must prepare for optimal community engagement.

REFERENCES

Butterfoss FD. *Coalitions and partnerships in community health.* San Francisco: Jossey-Bass; 2007.

Butterfoss FD, Kegler MC. The community coalition action theory. In: DiClemente RJ, Crosby RA, Kegler MC (editors). *Emerging theories in health promotion practice and research* (2nd ed., pp. 237-276). San Francisco: Jossey-Bass; 2009.

Centers for Disease Control and Prevention. *Essential public health services.* Atlanta (GA): Centers for Disease Control and Prevention; 1994.

Handler A, Issel M, Turnock B. A conceptual framework to measure performance of the public health system. *American Journal of Public Health* 2001;91(8):1235-1239.

Hatcher MT, Nicola RM. Building constituencies for public health. In: Novick LF, Morrow CB, Mays GP (editors). *Public health administration: principles for population-based management* (1st ed., pp. 510-520). Sudbury (MA): Jones and Bartlett; 2001.

Hatcher MT, Nicola RM. Building constituencies for public health. In: Novick LF, Morrow CB, Mays GP (editors). *Public health administration: principles for population-based management* (2nd ed., pp. 443-458). Sudbury (MA): Jones and Bartlett; 2008.

Kozel CT, Hubbell AP, Dearing JW, Kane WM, Thompson S, Pérez FG, et al. Exploring agenda-setting for healthy border 2010: research directions and methods. *Californian Journal of Health Promotion* 2006a;4(1):141-161.

Kozel C, Kane W, Hatcher M, Hubbell A, Dearing J, Forster-Cox S, et al. Introducing health promotion agenda-setting for health education practitioners. *Californian Journal of Health Promotion* 2006b;4(1):32-40.

Kozel C, Kane W, Rogers E, Brandon J, Hatcher M, Hammes M, et al. Exploring health promotion agenda-setting in New Mexico: reshaping health promotion leadership. *Promotion and Education* 2003;(4):171-177.

National Association of County and City Health Officials. Mobilizing for action through planning and partnerships (MAPP). National Association of County and City Health Officials; 2011. Retrieved from http://www.naccho.org/topics/infrastructure/MAPP/index.cfm.

Nicola RM, Hatcher MT. A framework for building effective public health constituencies. *Journal of Public Health Management and Practice* 2000;6(2):1-10.

Turnock BJ. *Public health: what it is and how it works* (4th ed.). Sudbury (MA): Jones and Bartlett; 2009.

APPENDIX 4.1 STRUCTURAL CAPACITY TABLES

The four tables listing the structural capacity needed for community engagement are shown here; one table has been constructed for each of the four practice elements (know the community, establish strategies, build networks, and mobilize communities). Each table includes summarized versions of the CCAT propositions and principles of community engagement that are relevant to the practice element represented by that table. CCAT propositions are displayed side-by-side with the principles to which they correspond. Both are numbered in accordance with their order in their original context. (For example, Principle 3 of our principles of community engagement is consistently identified in these tables as number 3 despite its location in the tables.)

The far-right column describes the structural capacity needed; these requirements are derived by considering the five elements of capacity set forth by Handler et al. (2001) in light of the CCAT propositions and engagement principles identified as relevant to each practice element.

Table 4.1. Know the Community, Its Constituents, and Its Capabilities[1]

Community Coalition Action Theory	Principles of Community Engagement	Structural Capacity Needed
Propositions: 3. All stages of coalition development are heavily influenced by community context. 4. Coalitions form in response to an opportunity, threat, or mandate. 5. Coalitions are more likely to form when the convening group provides technical/material/networking assistance and credibility. 6. Coalition formation is more likely when there is participation from community gatekeepers. 7. Coalition formation usually begins by recruiting a core group of people committed to resolving the issue. 8. More effective coalitions result when the core group expands to include participants who represent diverse interest groups. 15. Satisfied and committed members will participate more fully in the work of the coalition. 16. Synergistic pooling of resources promotes effective assessment, planning, and implementation. 17. Comprehensive assessment and planning aid successful implementation of effective strategies.	*Principles:* 2. Know the community, including its economics, demographics, norms, history, experience with engagement efforts, and perception of those initiating the engagement activities. 6. Recognize and respect the various cultures of a community and other factors that indicate its diversity in all aspects of designing and implementing community engagement approaches. 7. Sustainability results from identifying and mobilizing community assets and from developing capacities and resources. 9. Community collaboration requires long-term commitment.	*People Skilled in:* • Outreach, relationship building, data collection and analysis, and information development and presentation. • Technical assistance and assessment of training needs for organizational formation, planning and implementation of initiatives, communication and networking, and other engagement processes. • Situational analysis and identifying opportunities for reciprocity within the community. *Information/Data on:* • Community demographics. • Socioeconomic status. • Cultural beliefs, attitudes, and behaviors regarding health and other contextual aspects of community life. • Community civic, faith, business, philanthropic, governmental, and other special interest entities — their missions/purpose, assets, and opinion leaders. • Physical attributes of the community. *Organizational Structures to:* • Organizational mission or values statement that supports a culture of long-term engagement with community partners. • Recognition and reward systems for personnel who effectively perform duties of community information development. • Information systems to manage collection, storage, analysis, and reporting of data on the capabilities of community partners; technical assistance and training needs for partners to undertake the formation of engagements, planning of initiatives, and implementation; development and maintenance of communication channels and networks; and opportunities to take part in other engagement processes. • Policies and procedures regarding collection, storage, release, or publication of information, along with privacy and security safeguards. *Fiscal and Physical Support for:* • Personnel, contract, or budget for providing information services. • Budget for development and distribution of information materials. • Office space for staff engaged in information services. • Computer hardware, communication devices, and other office equipment.

Reprinted with permission of John Wiley & Sons, Inc.
References: Butterfoss, 2007; Butterfoss et al., 2009.
[1]CCAT propositions and the principles of community engagement are numbered in accordance with their order in their original context, not according to their position in this table.

Table 4.2. Establish Positions and Strategies to Guide Interactions[2]

Community Coalition Action Theory	Principles of Community Engagement	Structural Capacity Needed
Propositions: 4. Coalitions form in response to an opportunity, threat, or mandate. 7. Coalition formation usually begins by recruiting a core group of people committed to resolving the issue. 9. Open, frequent communication creates a positive climate for collaborative synergy. 10. Shared and formalized decision-making helps make collaborative synergy more likely through member engagement and pooling of resources. 12. Strong leadership improves coalition functioning and makes collaborative synergy more likely. 13. Paid staff with interpersonal and organizational skills can facilitate the collaborative process. 14. Formalized rules, roles, structures, and procedures make collaborative synergy more likely. 16. Synergistic pooling of resources promotes effective assessment, planning, and implementation. 17. Comprehensive assessment and planning aid successful implementation of effective strategies. 18. Coalitions that direct interventions at multiple levels are more likely to create change in community policies, practices, and environments.	*Principles:* 1. Be clear about the population/ communities to be engaged and the goals of the effort. 4. Remember that community self-determination is the responsibility and right of all people who comprise a community. 6. Recognize and respect the various cultures of a community and other factors that indicate its diversity in all aspects of designing and implementing community engagement approaches. 8. Be prepared to release control to the community, and be flexible enough to meet the changing needs of the community. 9. Community collaboration requires long-term commitment.	*People Skilled in:* • Information and policy analysis, strategic planning and strategy development, and initiative planning and implementation. • Collaborative methods to work with diverse populations and build community capacity to analyze and apply information in decision making. • Affiliation and network linkage development, organizational formation, collaborative leadership, facilitation, and participatory governance. • Resource identification and leveraged resource management. • Communications development and delivery. *Information/Data on:* • Populations potentially affected by positions under consideration and influencing factors of socioeconomic, cultural, and other situational/ contextual data. • Population response anticipated based on beliefs, attitudes, past behaviors, and readiness to act and participate. • Opportunities to engage opinion leaders in position and strategy determination. • Symbols, physical location, institutions, and events likely to improve engagement. *Organizational Structures to:* • Establish information systems to obtain formative information on issues for which community engagement is needed. • Analyze the range of solutions or actions, unintended consequences, and the opportunities to successfully address the issue(s) where community engagement is intended. • Project resource needs and potential ways to attract, leverage, and manage resources. • Determine organizational position and strategies to initiate community dialogue on perceived issues. • Present positions and negotiate consensus on community actions or what outcomes to achieve. • Recognize and reward personnel that effectively perform community engagement and strategy development duties. *Fiscal and Physical Support for:* • Personnel budget for strategic and program planning. • Personnel budget for facilitating development of community capacity to act. • Budget for strategic and program planning. • Office space for staff engaged in strategic and program planning. • Communication and computer hardware and other office equipment to support position and strategy development activities.

Reprinted with permission of John Wiley & Sons, Inc.
References: Butterfoss, 2007; Butterfoss et al., 2009.
[2]CCAT propositions and the principles of community engagement are numbered in accordance with their order in their original context, not according to their position in this table.

Table 4.3. Build and Sustain Networks to Maintain Relationships, Communications, and Leveraging of Resources[3]

Community Coalition Action Theory	Principles of Community Engagement	Structural Capacity Needed
Propositions: 5. Coalitions are more likely to form when the convening group provides technical/material/networking assistance and credibility. 6. Coalition formation is more likely when there is participation from community gatekeepers. 7. Coalition formation usually begins by recruiting a core group of people committed to resolving the issue. 8. More effective coalitions result when the core group expands to include participants who represent diverse interest groups. 9. Open, frequent communication creates a positive climate for collaborative synergy. 12. Strong leadership improves coalition functioning and makes collaborative synergy more likely. 13. Paid staff with interpersonal and organizational skills can facilitate the collaborative process. 15. Satisfied and committed members will participate more fully in the work of the coalition. 16. Synergistic pooling of resources promotes effective assessment, planning, and implementation. 17. Comprehensive assessment and planning aid successful implementation of effective strategies.	**Principles:** 3. To create community mobilization process, build trust and relationships and get commitments from formal and informal leadership. 7. Sustainability results from identifying and mobilizing community assets and from developing capacities and resources. 9. Community collaboration requires long-term commitment.	**People Skilled in:** • Network analysis and affiliation processes, engagement processes that respect diverse populations and viewpoints, collaborative leadership, network formation and ethical management of asymmetrical power relationships, resource identification and leveraged resource management, and communications development and delivery. **Information/Data on:** • Network demographics and socioeconomic status. • Network cultural beliefs, attitudes, and behaviors regarding health and other aspects of community life. • Network structures and opinion leaders within these structures. • Network "boundary-spanners" who provide linkage across population and system segments of the community. **Organizational Structures to:** • Recognize and reward personnel who effectively perform community engagement network duties. • Identify and understand the patterns of communication, influence, and resource flow. • Establish information systems to manage and maintain trusted two-way network communication. • Encourage personnel to affiliate with formal and informal organizations and groups across the community and leverage those affiliation points to support the organization's network structures (communication, power/influence, and resource flow). • Establish information systems to support network formation and affiliation processes, network planning and implementation, and network resource identification and leveraged management. • Oversee communications and policy-related activities needed to leverage resources within the network structure. • Establish, use, and monitor resource exchange systems that support network interactions and coordinated community collaborative work. **Fiscal and Physical Support for:** • Personnel budget for network development and maintenance. • Personnel budget to support and reward personnel performance in network development and maintenance. • Office space for staff engaged in network development and maintenance. • Communication and computer hardware and other office equipment to support mobilization activities.

Reprinted with permission of John Wiley & Sons, Inc.
References: Butterfoss, 2007; Butterfoss et al., 2009.
[3]CCAT propositions and the principles of community engagement are numbered in accordance with their order in their original context, not according to their position in this table.

Table 4.4. Mobilize Communities and Constituencies for Decision Making and Social Action[4]

Community Coalition Action Theory	Principles of Community Engagement	Structural Capacity Needed
Propositions: 6. Coalition formation is more likely when there is participation from community gatekeepers. 7. Coalition formation usually begins by recruiting a core group of people committed to resolving the issue. 10. Shared and formalized decision-making helps make collaborative synergy more likely through member engagement and pooling of resources. 11. Conflict management helps create a positive organizational climate, ensures that benefits outweigh costs, and achieves pooling of resources and member engagement. 12. Strong leadership improves coalition functioning and makes collaborative synergy more likely. 13. Paid staff with interpersonal and organizational skills can facilitate the collaborative process. 14. Formalized rules, roles, structures, and procedures make collaborative synergy more likely. 15. Satisfied and committed members will participate more fully in the work of the coalition. 16. Synergistic pooling of resources promotes effective assessment, planning, and implementation. 17. Comprehensive assessment and planning aid successful implementation of effective strategies. 18. Coalitions that direct interventions at multiple levels are more likely to create change in community policies, practices, and environments.	*Principles:* 4. Remember and accept that community self-determination is the responsibility and right of all people who comprise a community. No external entity should assume it could bestow to a community the power to act in its own self-interest. 5. Partnering with the community is necessary to create change and improve health. 6. Recognize and respect the various cultures of a community and other factors that indicate its diversity in all aspects of designing and implementing community engagement approaches. 7. Sustainability results from identifying and mobilizing community assets and from developing capacities and resources. 8. Be prepared to release control to the community, and be flexible enough to meet the changing needs of the community. 9. Community collaboration requires long-term commitment.	*People Skilled in:* • Mobilization and engagement processes, execution of mobilization strategies, initiative planning and implementation, collaborative organizational formation and participatory governance, listening, appreciating diverse populations and viewpoints, collaborative leadership to ethically manage asymmetric power relationships, resource identification, and leveraged resource management, and communications development and delivery. • Technical assistance and training to build partner capacity to participate in community actions. *Information/Data on:* • Emerging or new competitive viewpoints and cultural beliefs, attitudes, and behaviors regarding health and other aspects of community life. • Shifts in community structures and opinions of leaders within these structures. • Impacts of engagement and mobilization efforts *Organizational Structures to:* • Collectively govern the collaborative process and communicate effectively with community partners. • Establish information systems to manage and maintain trusted two-way network communication. • Establish information systems to support affiliations and mobilization process of engagement initiatives, contingency planning to adapt implementation of collaborative interventions, and feedback on use and management of network resources. • Deliver technical assistance and training. • Establish information systems to provide feedback loops to evaluate impacts of engagement and intervention mobilization efforts. • Track personnel affiliated with formal and informal organizations and groups across the community. • Leverage affiliation points to support the organization's network and mobilization activities (communication, power/influence, resource flow, and collaborative interventions). • Oversee communications and policy-related activities network and mobilization activities. • Manage resource exchange needed to accomplish coordinated community collaborative work. • Recognize and reward personnel that effectively perform community engagement and social mobilization duties. *Fiscal and Physical Support for:* • Personnel budget for managing and evaluating mobilization activities that address active communication, power relationships, resource flow and use, and other collaborative processes. • Personnel budget to support and reward personnel performance in managing and evaluating mobilization activities. • Office space for staff engaged in managing and evaluating mobilization activities. • Communication and computer hardware and other office equipment to support mobilization activities.

Reprinted with permission of John Wiley & Sons, Inc.
References: Butterfoss, 2007; Butterfoss et al., 2009.
[4]CCCAT propositions and the principles of community engagement are numbered in accordance with their order in their original context, not according to their position in this table.

5

Challenges in Improving Community Engagement in Research

Chapter 5
Challenges in Improving Community Engagement in Research

Jo Anne Grunbaum, EdD

INTRODUCTION

This chapter addresses common challenges faced in community-engaged research, whether that research meets the definition of community-based participatory research (CBPR) or falls elsewhere on the spectrum of community engagement efforts. These challenges and some approaches for meeting them are illustrated with a series of vignettes that describe real-life experiences of partnerships emanating from the Prevention Research Centers (PRC) program, the Clinical and Translational Science Awards (CTSA) program, and other community-engaged research (CEnR) efforts.

CDC funds PRCs in schools of public health and medicine; the first three PRCs were funded in 1986. Currently, 37 PRCs are funded across 27 states, working as an interdependent network of community, academic, and public health partners to conduct applied prevention research and support the wide use of practices proven to promote good health. These partners design, test, and disseminate strategies that can be implemented as new policies or recommended public health practices. For more information on the PRC program, visit www.cdc.gov/prc.

The CTSA program began in 2006 with 12 sites funded by the National Center for Research Resources, a part of NIH. As of publication, the CTSA Consortium includes 55 medical research institutions located throughout the nation that work together to energize the discipline of clinical and translational science. The CTSA institutions share a common vision to improve human health by transforming the research and training environment in the U.S. to enhance the efficiency and quality of clinical and translational research. Community engagement programs in the CTSAs help foster collaborative and interdisciplinary research partnerships, enhance public trust in clinical and translational research, and facilitate the recruitment and retention of research participants to learn more about health issues in the United States' many diverse populations. For more information on the CTSA Consortium, visit www.CTSAweb.org.

The purpose of this chapter is to address five key challenges in the area of community-engaged research:

1. Engaging and maintaining community involvement.

2. Overcoming differences between and among academics and the community.

3. Working with nontraditional communities.

4. Initiating a project with a community and developing a community advisory board.

5. Overcoming competing priorities and institutional differences.

Each vignette describes a challenge faced by a partnership and the actions taken and provides pertinent take-home messages. The intention is to provide readers with snapshots of community engagement activity during the research process. Readers are encouraged to contact the authors or refer to the references for further information concerning findings and follow-up.

1. ENGAGING AND MAINTAINING COMMUNITY INVOLVEMENT

Many communities distrust the motives and techniques of research. Some know of the history of exploitation and abuse in medical research in the U.S., and others may be "burned out" from participation in studies. Some may have immediate needs that make research seem irrelevant, and some may merely lack an understanding of the research enterprise.

Thus, when research is involved, the challenges of community engagement may be particularly profound. The vignettes that follow address some of the most common dilemmas in engaging a community in research and maintaining the relationship over time. The take-home messages offered at the end of each vignette are grounded in the principles of community engagement, as they demonstrate the importance of understanding communities; establishing trusting, respectful, equitable, and committed relationships; and working with the community to identify the best ways to translate knowledge into improved health.

A. How do you engage a community in a randomized clinical trial or a drug trial?

Sally Davis, PhD

Challenge

Community-based research does not always allow for full participation of the community from start to finish, as is envisioned in the classic CBPR model. In CBPR, the community often comes up with the research question or issue of interest based on personal experience, but in a randomized controlled trial (RCT), the funding agency or investigator generally develops the question based on pressing health issues identified from surveillance or other data sources. A community-based RCT is often an efficacy trial and may include many schools or communities across a large geographic area.

For example, the PRC at the University of New Mexico conducted an RCT on obesity prevention with 16 rural Head Start centers across the state. An RCT conducted in the traditional way is done in an artificial "laboratory" setting within an academic health center or practice setting; an RCT in the community setting can be just as rigorous but with more flexibility and community participation. The challenge has been to develop strategies to engage the community in the research process within a short period of time and with clear communication and agreement.

Action Steps

Although the study was conducted in 16 communities and there was little time to establish relationships, researchers were able to engage the communities by inviting key partners to participate. For example, local grocery stores, health care providers, families, Head Start teachers, teaching assistants, and food-service providers were all included. This inclusive approach ensured participation from a broad array of community members from the beginning of the study. A memorandum of agreement (MOA) was developed that included input from community leaders and provided an opportunity for the researchers and the community to discuss and agree on roles, responsibilities, and expectations. Key members of the community (e.g., governing officials, school administration, and parent groups) and the university researchers signed the agreement. The MOA includes a clear statement of the purpose of the research, burden to the school or individual (the amount of time required to participate), benefits to the school (money, equipment, in-kind service), benefits to the academic institution and researchers (the opportunity to answer important questions and test interventions), needs (space, parental consent, special events, identification of other key individuals), and communication issues (regarding scheduling, staff turnover, complaints). The MOA is being used as a guidance document for the study. Having this agreement in writing is especially helpful when there is turnover of key participants, such as school staff or governing officials, or when there are new participants who may not be aware of the history or purpose of the study or of the roles, relationships, and responsibilities agreed upon at the beginning of the research.

> This inclusive approach ensured participation from a broad array of community members from the beginning of the study.

Take-Home Messages

- Engaging the community in RCTs is challenging but possible.

- Engaging and seeking input from multiple key stakeholders (e.g., grocery store owners, health care providers, and families) is an important strategy.

- Collaboratively developing an MOA can enhance communication and build new partnerships in studies that are restricted by time and are predefined.

- An MOA can serve as a valuable guidance document and useful tool throughout a study as an agreed-upon point of reference for researchers and community members (Davis et al., 1999; Davis et al., 2003).

References

Davis SM, Clay T, Smyth M, Gittelsohn J, Arviso V, Flint-Wagner H, et al. Pathways curriculum and family interventions to promote healthful eating and physical activity in American Indian schoolchildren. *Preventive Medicine* 2003;37(6 Part 2):S24-34.

Davis SM, Going SB, Helitzer DL, Teufel NI, Snyder P, Gittelsohn J, et al. Pathways: a culturally appropriate obesity-prevention program for American Indian schoolchildren. *American Journal of Clinical Nutrition* 1999;69(4 Suppl):796S-802S.

B. How do you overcome historical exploitation?

Sally Davis, PhD, Janet Page-Reeves, PhD, Theresa Cruz, PhD

Challenge

A history of exploitation in rural communities may be manifested in a number of ways. In many such communities, structural inequality is evident in residents' geographic isolation, great distance from commercial centers, lack of access to services, lack of availability of healthful foods, and poverty, as well as frequent turnover of staff in local institutions such as schools and health care facilities. This reality presents everyday challenges to the researchers at institutions that work in these communities. For example, distance, weather, and lack of infrastructure pose logistical challenges, and a lack of road maintenance, limited communication capacity, and uncertain access to food and lodging (necessities that urban residents may take for granted) are often problems in rural areas. These issues, combined with the problem of scheduling around competing priorities in the lives of both researchers and community members, are challenges for those living in or working with rural communities.

These challenges do not compare, however, with those created by the historical exploitation of residents in some of these communities. In the Southwest, where research has too often been conducted in an exploitative manner without the consent and participation of the community, it is extremely difficult to develop partnerships between rural communities and researchers. Many American Indian and Hispanic communities throughout the Southwest have been the subjects of research conducted by persons living outside the community who did not engage residents and their communities in the research. In one multisite study with tribal groups across the United States that began in the 1990s, researchers at the University of New Mexico PRC and at four other universities were confronted with the challenge of overcoming the mistrust of seven tribal communities that had either experienced exploitation or heard of examples.

Action Steps

Despite the history of violated trust, the PRC was able to develop appropriate and meaningful partnerships between researchers and tribal communities. Together, the partners established and maintained the bidirectional trust necessary to develop and implement a successful intervention. They used a variety of participation strategies to achieve trust. For example, local customs and cultural constructs were considered in formulating the intervention, local advisory councils were formed, elders were included as advisors, local community members were hired, formative assessment was conducted to determine the feasibility and acceptability of the proposed prevention strategies in local terms, approval was sought from tribal and local review boards, and local priorities were determined. Participation, feedback, and collaborative relationships were crucial to engaging these underrepresented communities with a history of exploitation. And yet, perhaps the most important and most basic strategy was to demonstrate respect and inclusion to the fullest extent possible.

> Together, the partners established and maintained the bidirectional trust necessary to develop and implement a successful intervention.

Take-Home Messages

- Recognize that there may be a history of exploitation in the community and therefore a distrust of research and researchers.

- Employ a variety of participation strategies.

- Allow extra time for building relationships and trust.

- Seek approval from tribal or other local review groups.

- Include local customs in interventions.

- Demonstrate respect and inclusion to the fullest extent possible (Davis et al., 1999; Gittelsohn et al., 2003).

References

Davis SM, Reid R. Practicing participatory research in American Indian communities. *American Society for Clinical Nutrition* 1999;69(4 Suppl):755S-759S.

Gittelsohn J, Davis SM, Steckler A, Ethelbah B, Clay T, Metcalfe L, et al. Pathways: lessons learned and future directions for school-based interventions among American Indians. *Preventive Medicine* 2003;37(6):S107-S112.

C. How do you maintain community engagement throughout the research?

Deborah Bowen, PhD

Challenge

The comedian Woody Allen once said, "Eighty percent of life is showing up." That is true in community engagement as well as in life. Add to that formula the idea of showing up for the right events — those that are important to community priorities — and engagement takes place. For example, the author's research group was funded to conduct a feasibility study of using rural farm granges as health promotion sites in ranching country. Granges are rural community organizations that support learning, information exchange, social events, and political action for farming and ranching communities. The feasibility study progressed from initial discussions to collection of formative data. These data collection efforts were by telephone, and, at first, response rates from the actual membership were relatively poor. The research group halted its efforts to collect data and conducted some qualitative research to better understand the issues.

Action Steps

The researchers found that lack of familiarity with the author's research institute and the people involved might be one barrier to full participation of the rural residents and grange members. Over the next six months, the research institute staff began to attend community and farming events, getting to know residents and families and learning what the community's important issues were. Research institute staff asked about these issues and attended events or supported efforts in the farming communities that were not necessarily related to health promotion but were key to the farm families in the granges. Several farm family members became part of the project's community advisory board, giving both advice and direction to the new plans for surveys. After six months, the research group, together with the community advisory board, reinstated the telephone data collection efforts, which then achieved a much higher response rate. This kind of community engagement continued for the three-year project. These same connections with farm families in granges are still fueling health promotion efforts in this area.

> The researchers found that lack of familiarity with the author's research institute and the people involved might be one barrier to full participation of the rural residents and grange members.

Take-Home Messages

- Engagement needs to occur as the ideas for research are being formed and the procedures are being identified.

- Taking the community's priorities into account increases the opportunity for engagement.

- Being a regular presence in the community may enhance research efforts.

D. How do you engage a community organization as a partner in exploratory health research?

Lori Carter-Edwards, PhD, Ashley Johnson, Lesley Williams, Janelle Armstrong-Brown, MPH

Challenge

The John Avery Boys and Girls Club (JABGC), located in the heart of a low-to-lower-middle-income community in Durham, North Carolina, primarily serves African American children and their families by providing a variety of after-school programs and activities. The organization is partnering with the Duke Center for Community Research (DCCR) to conduct a qualitative exploratory research study to understand children's influences on the food purchasing behaviors of caregivers in the context of food marketing. African American children have a much higher prevalence of obesity than children of other ethnic groups (Skelton et al., 2009) and are more likely than other children to receive targeted marketing messages for products associated with intake of excess calories (Grier et al., 2010; Kumanyika et al., 2006). The intent of this study is to gain information on the local food environment to help inform and ultimately to modify policy. JABGC had a previous relationship with DCCR personnel in the area of program and policy development, but this was its first experience serving as a full partner with the DCCR in research.

Action Steps

The DCCR and the JABGC have met regularly since the development and funding of the study, which is sponsored by the African-American Collaborative Obesity Research Network, a national research network based at the University of Pennsylvania through a grant from the Robert Wood Johnson Foundation. The executive director of the JABGC identified an administrative lead from the club to serve as its point person. The DCCR faculty lead for the study and other researchers frequently visit the JABGC and have established a rapport with its entire administrative and programmatic staff. The core partners hold weekly telephone meetings to address issues related to execution of the study. During some calls, partners have discussed the data that needed to be collected and why, and these discussions helped to dramatically improve documentation. Regular telephone meetings also helped to clarify job priorities. It was important that the DCCR partners understood the work priorities of the JABGC staff and the limitations of what could and could not be accomplished during the study.

Some of the JABGC administrative staff has changed since the research began, but because of the rapport built through the partnership and the existing mechanisms for communication, the changes have not adversely affected the team's ability to conduct the research. Continued communications between the DCCR and the JABGC administrative and programmatic staff have been key to sustaining organizational relationships.

Take-Home Messages

- Establishing a collaborative research relationship may involve a different level of engagement than a collaborative outreach relationship.

- Organizations have their own responsibilities that have to be met independently of any research.

- Communicating regularly and often to keep all partners aware of priorities within the respective institutions is important.

- Working collectively to proactively create relationships and put procedures in place can help sustain the research when the community organization staff changes.

- It should be understood that, despite the time limits for research, partnerships must be flexible.

References

Grier SA, Kumanyika S. Targeted marketing and public health. *Annual Review of Public Health* 2010;31:349-369.

Kumanyika S, Grier S. Targeting interventions for ethnic minority and low-income populations. *The Future of Children* 2006;16(1):187-207.

Skelton JA, Cook SR, Auinger P, Klein JD, Barlow SE. Prevalence and trends of severe obesity among US children and adolescents. *Academic Pediatrics* 2009;9(5):322-329.

2. OVERCOMING DIFFERENCES BETWEEN AND AMONG ACADEMICS AND THE COMMUNITY

The backgrounds and languages of researchers are often different from those of community members. The concept of culture noted in Chapter 1 captures the different norms that can govern the attitudes and behaviors of researchers and those who are not part of the research enterprise. In addition, the inequalities highlighted by the socio-ecological perspective often manifest in difficult "town-gown" relationships. How can these differences be overcome in the interests of CEnR?

A. How do you engage the community when there are cultural differences (race or ethnicity) between the community and the researchers?

Kimberly Horn, EdD, Geri Dino, PhD

Challenge

American Indian youth are one of the demographic groups at highest risk for smoking (Johnston et al., 2002; CDC, 2006), and yet there is little research regarding effective interventions for American Indian teens to prevent or quit smoking. Unfortunately, American Indians have a long history of negative experiences with research, ranging from being exploited by this research to being ignored by researchers. Specifically, they have been minimally involved in research on tobacco addiction and cessation in their own communities. This problem is compounded by the economic, spiritual, and cultural significance of tobacco in American Indian culture. In the late 1990s, the West Virginia University PRC and its partners were conducting research on teen smoking cessation in North Carolina, largely among white teens. Members of the North Carolina American Indian community approached the researchers about addressing smoking among American Indian teens, focusing on state-recognized tribes.

Action Steps

CBPR approaches can be particularly useful when working with underserved communities, such as American Indians, who have historically been exploited. For this reason, CBPR approaches served as the framework for a partnership that included the West Virginia University PRC, the North Carolina Commission of Indian Affairs, the eight state-recognized tribes, and the University of North Carolina PRC. The CBPR-driven process began with formation of a multi-tribe community partnership board composed of tribal leaders, parents, teachers, school personnel, and clergy. The researchers and the community board developed a document of shared values to guide the research process. Community input regarding the nature of the program was obtained from focus groups, interviews, surveys, and informal discussions, including testimonials and numerous venues for historical storytelling.

> The researchers and the community board developed a document of shared values to guide the research process.

As the community and the researchers continued to meet, they encountered challenges concerning the role and meaning of tobacco in American Indian culture. The researchers saw tobacco as the problem, but many community members did not share that view. This was a significant issue to resolve before the project could move forward. A major breakthrough occurred when the partners reached a declarative insight that *tobacco addiction,* not tobacco, was the challenge to be addressed. From that day forward, the group agreed to develop a program on smoking cessation for teens that specifically addressed tobacco addiction from a cultural perspective. In addition, the community decided to use the evidence-based Not on Tobacco (N-O-T) program developed by the West Virginia University PRC as the starting point. American Indian smokers and nonsmokers, N-O-T facilitators from North Carolina, and the community board all provided input into the program's development. In addition, teen smokers provided session-by-session feedback on the original N-O-T program. Numerous recommendations for tailoring and modifying N-O-T resulted in a new N-O-T curriculum for American Indians. The adaptation now provides 10 tailored sessions (Horn et al., 2005a; Horn et al., 2008).

The N-O-T program as modified for American Indians continues to be used in North Carolina, and there are ongoing requests from various tribes across the U.S. for information about the program. The initial partnership was supported by goodwill and good faith, and the partnership between American Indians and N-O-T led to additional collaborations, including a three-year CDC-funded CBPR project to further test the American Indian N-O-T program and to alter the political and cultural norms related to tobacco across North Carolina tribes. Critically, grant resources were divided almost equally among the West Virginia PRC, the North Carolina PRC, and the North Carolina Commission on Indian Affairs. Each organization had monetary control over its resources. In addition, all grants included monies to be distributed to community members and tribes for their participation. This statewide initiative served as a springboard for localized planning and action for tobacco control and prevention across North Carolina tribes (Horn et al., 2005b).

Take-Home Messages

- Act on the basis of value-driven, community-based principles, which assure recognition of a community-driven need.

- Build on the strengths and assets of the community of interest.

- Nurture partnerships in all project phases; partnership is iterative.

- Integrate the cultural knowledge of the community.

- Produce mutually beneficial tools and products.

- Build capacity through co-learning and empowerment.

- Share all findings and knowledge with all partners.

References

Centers for Disease Control and Prevention. Cigarette smoking among adults—United States, 2006. *Morbidity and Mortality Weekly Report* 2007;56(44):1157-1161.

Horn K, Dino G, Goldcamp J, Kalsekar I, Mody R. The impact of Not On Tobacco on teen smoking cessation: end-of-program evaluation results, 1998 to 2003. *Journal of Adolescent Research* 2005a;20(6):640-661.

Horn K, McCracken L, Dino G, Brayboy M. Applying community-based participatory research principles to the development of a smoking-cessation program for American Indian teens: "telling our story." *Health Education and Behavior* 2008;35(1):44-69.

Horn K, McGloin T, Dino G, Manzo K, McCracken L, Shorty L, et al. Quit and reduction rates for a pilot study of the American Indian Not On Tobacco (N-O-T) program. *Preventing Chronic Disease* 2005b;2(4):A13.

Johnston L, O'Malley P, Bachman J. *Monitoring the future national survey results on drug use, 1975–2002.* NIH Publication No.03-5375. Bethesda (MD): National Institute on Drug Abuse; 2002.

B. How do you work with a community when there are educational or sociodemographic differences between the community and the researchers?

Marc A. Zimmerman, PhD, E. Hill De Loney, MA

Challenge

University and community partners often have different social, historical, and economic backgrounds, which can create tension, miscommunication, and misunderstanding. These issues were evident in a recent submission of a grant proposal; all of the university partners had advanced degrees, came from European-American backgrounds, and grew up with economic security. In contrast, the backgrounds of the community partners ranged from two years of college to nearing completion of a Ph.D., and socioeconomic backgrounds were varied. All of the community partners were involved in a community-based organization and came from African American backgrounds.

Despite extensive discussion and a participatory process (e.g., data-driven dialogue and consensus about the final topic selected), the community-university partnership was strained during the writing of the proposal. Time was short, and the university partners volunteered to outline the contents of the proposal, identify responsibilities for writing different parts of the proposal, and begin writing. The proposal details (e.g., design, contents of the intervention, recruitment strategy, and comparison community) were discussed mostly through conference calls.

Action Steps

The university partners began writing, collating what others wrote, and initiating discussions of (and pushing for) specific design elements. Recruitment strategy became a point of contention and led to heavy discussion. The university partners argued that a more scientifically sound approach would be to recruit individuals from clinic settings that had no prior connections to those individuals. The community partners argued that a more practical and locally sound approach would be to recruit through their personal networks. No resolution came during the telephone calls, and so the university partners discussed among themselves the two sides of the argument and decided to write the first draft with participants recruited from clinic settings (in accord with their original position). The university partners sent the draft to the entire group, including the county health department and a local health coalition as well as the community partners, for comments.

The community partners did not respond to drafts of the proposal as quickly as the university partners expected, given the deadlines and administrative work that were required to get the proposal submitted through the university. This lack of response was interpreted by the university partners as tacit approval, especially given the tight deadline. However, the silence of the community partners turned out to be far from an expression of approval. Their impression, based on the fact that the plan was already written and time was getting shorter, was that the university partners did not really want feedback. They also felt that they were not respected because their ideas were not included in the proposal. The university partners, however, sincerely meant their document as a draft and wanted the community partners' feedback about the design. They thought there was still time to change some aspects of the proposal before its final approval and submission by the partnership. The tight deadline, the scientific convictions of the university partners, the reliance on telephone communications, and the imbalance of power between the partners all contributed to the misunderstanding and miscommunication about the design. This process created significant problems that have taken time to address and to heal.

Take-Home Messages

- Be explicit that drafts mean that changes can be made and that feedback is both expected and desired.

- Have more face-to-face meetings, especially when discussing points about which there may be disagreement, because telephone conferencing does not allow for nonverbal cues and makes it more difficult to disagree.

- Figure out ways to be scientifically sound in locally appropriate ways.

- Acknowledge and discuss power imbalances.

- Ensure that all partners' voices are heard and listened to, create settings for open and honest discussion, and communicate perspectives clearly.

- Help partners understand when they are being disrespectful or might be misinterpreted.

- Discuss differences even after a proposal is submitted.

- Improve communication by establishing agreed-upon deadlines and midpoint check-ins, using active listening strategies, specifically requesting feedback with time frames, and facing issues directly so that everyone understands them.

- Provide community partners with time and opportunity for developing designs for proposals, and provide training for community partners if they lack knowledge in some areas of research design.

- Set aside time for university partners to learn about the community partners' knowledge of the community and what expertise they bring to a specific project.

- Acknowledge expertise within the partnership explicitly and take advantage of it when necessary.

C. How do you engage a community when there are cultural, educational, or socioeconomic differences within the community as well as between the community and the researchers?

Seronda A. Robinson, PhD, Wanda A. Boone, RN, Sherman A. James, PhD, Mina Silberberg, PhD, Glenda Small, MBA

Challenge

Conducting community-engaged research requires overcoming various hierarchies to achieve a common goal. Hierarchies may be created by differing economic status, social affiliation, education, or position in the workplace or the community. A Pew Research Center survey, described by Kohut et al. (2007), suggests that the values of poor and middle-class African Americans have moved farther apart from each other in recent years and that middle-class African Americans' values have become more like those of whites than of poor African Americans. In addition, African Americans are reporting seeing greater differences created by class than by race (Kohut et al. 2007). It is widely known that perceived differences in values may influence interactions between groups.

Approaches to engage the community can be used as bridge builders when working with economically divided groups. The African-American Health Improvement Partnership (AAHIP) was launched in October 2005 in Durham, North Carolina, with a grant from the National Center (now Institute) for Minority Health and Health Disparities through a grant program focused on community participation. The AAHIP research team consists of African American and white researchers from Duke University with terminal degrees and research experience and health professionals/community advocates from the Community Health Coalition, Inc, a local nonprofit. The community advisory board (CAB) is composed of mostly African American community leaders representing diverse sectors of Durham's African American and health provider communities. The first study launched by the AAHIP, which is ongoing, is an intervention designed by the AAHIP CAB and its research team to improve disease management in African American adults with type 2 diabetes.

> Approaches to engage the community can be used as bridge builders when working with economically divided groups.

At meetings of the CAB, decisions were to be made by a majority vote of a quorum of its members. Members of the research team would serve as facilitators who provided guidance and voiced suggestions. The sharing of information was understood to be key to the process. However, dissimilarities in educational level and experience between the research team and the CAB and variations in socioeconomic status, positions, and community roles among CAB members created underlying hierarchies within the group (i.e., the CAB plus the research team). The research team assumed a leadership role in making recommendations. Notably, even within the CAB, differences among its members led to varying levels of comfort with the CAB process with the result that some members did most of the talking while others were hesitant to make contributions. Many of the community leaders were widely known for their positions within the community and their accomplishments, and these individuals were accustomed to voicing their opinions, being heard, and then being followed. Less influential members were not as assertive.

Action Steps

Faculty from North Carolina Central University, a historically black university in Durham, conduct annual evaluations to assess the functioning of the CAB and the research team, in particular to ensure that it is performing effectively and meeting the principles of CBPR. An early survey found that only about 10% of respondents felt that racial differences interfered with productivity, and 19% felt that the research team dominated the meetings. However, nearly half felt that the meetings were dominated by just one or a few members. Although more than 90% reported feeling comfortable expressing their point of view at the meetings, it was suggested that there was a need to get everyone involved.

CAB members suggested ways to rectify the issues of perceived dominance, and all parties agreed to the suggestions. From then on, the entire CAB membership was asked to contribute to the CAB meeting agendas as a way to offer a larger sense of inclusion. At the meetings themselves, the chair made a point of soliciting remarks from all CAB members until they became more comfortable speaking up without being prompted. In addition, subcommittees were established to address important business. These made active participation easier because of the size of the group.

As seats came open on the CAB, members were recruited with an eye to balancing representation in the group by various characteristics, including gender, age, socioeconomic status, and experience with diabetes (the outcome of interest). Overall, a change was seen in the level of participation at meetings, with more members participating and less dominance by a few. Moreover, former participants in the type 2 diabetes intervention were invited to join the CAB and have now assumed leadership roles.

Take-Home Messages

- Evaluate your process on an ongoing basis and discuss results as a group.

- Assure recognition of a community-driven need through strong and fair leadership.

- Make concerted efforts to draw out and acknowledge the voices of all participants.

- Create specialized committees.

- Engage participants in the choosing of new board members (especially former participants).

Reference

Kohut A, Taylor P, Keeter S. Optimism about black progress declines: blacks see growing values gap between poor and middle class. *Pew Social Trends Report* 2007;91. Retrieved from http://pewsocialtrends.org/files/2010/10/Race-2007.pdf.

3. WORKING WITH NONTRADITIONAL COMMUNITIES

As described in Chapter 1, communities vary greatly in their composition. New communication technologies mean that increasingly there are communities that do not conform to geographic boundaries and that collaboration can occur across great distances. These new kinds of communities and collaborations have their own unique challenges, illustrated in the following vignettes.

A. How do you maintain community engagement when the community is geographically distant from the researchers?

Deborah Bowen, PhD

Challenge

Distance poses a sometimes insurmountable barrier to open and accurate communication and engagement. People may feel left out if they perceive that distance is interfering with the connections between the research team and partners in the community. Maintaining involvement in multiple ways can solve this problem.

The principal investigator (PI) of an NIH-funded project was located at an academic institution, whereas community partners (Alaskan Natives and American Indians) were scattered through 40 sites across a large region in the U.S. Before the project began, the PI knew that even with an initial positive response, participation in the project would be hard to maintain across a multiyear project. She used two strategies to maintain contact and connection with the 40 community partners: refinements in organization and strategic personal visits.

Action Steps

The PI identified each community organization's preferred method for communication and used that method for regular scheduled contacts. The methods were mostly electronic (telephone, email, or fax). Every scheduled contact brought a communication from the contact person in the community, no matter how insignificant. The community partners contributed to the communication, and if they had an issue they communicated it to the contact person. The communications were used to solve all kinds of problems, not just those that were research related. In fact, communications were social and became sources of support as well as sources of project information. This contact with the 40 community partners was continued for the duration of the six-year project.

The PI knew that relying on electronic communication alone was not sufficient. Thus, despite the vast distances between her institution and the community partners, the PI scheduled at least annual visits to see them. She asked each partner for the most important meeting or event of the year and tried to time the visit to attend it. The face-to-face interaction allowed by these visits was meaningful to the PI and the partners. The PI followed the cultural rules of visits (e.g., bringing gifts from their region to the community partners). Even with the barriers of space and time, engagement at a personal level made the research activities easier and more memorable for the partners.

> The face-to-face interaction allowed by these visits was meaningful to the PI and the partners.

Take-Home Messages

- Take communication seriously, even if it is inconvenient to do so.

- Keep notes or files on the people involved to remember key events.

- Take into consideration the community partner's perspective on what is important.

Reference

Hill TG, Briant KJ, Bowen D, Boerner V, Vu T, Lopez K, Vinson E. Evaluation of Cancer 101: an educational program for native settings. *Journal of Cancer Education* 2010;25(3):329-336.

B. How do you engage a state as a community?

Geri Dino, PhD, Elizabeth Prendergast, MS, Valerie Frey-McClung, MS, Bruce Adkins, PA, Kimberly Horn, EdD

Challenge

West Virginia is the second most rural state in the U.S. with a population density of just 75 persons per square mile. The state consistently has one of the worst health profiles in the nation, including a disproportionably high burden of risk factors for chronic disease. The most notable is tobacco use (Trust for America's Health, 2008). Addressing these chronic disease risk disparities was central to West Virginia University's application to become a CDC-funded PRC. Early in the application process, senior leadership from the university engaged the state's public health and education partners to create a vision for the PRC. Both then and now, the PRC's state and community partners view West Virginia as having a culture of cooperation and service that embraces the opportunity to solve problems collectively. The vision that emerged, which continues to this day, reflected both the state's need and a sense of shared purpose — the entire state of West Virginia would serve as the Center's target community. Importantly, the academic-state partners committed themselves to develop the PRC as the state leader in prevention research by transforming public health policy and practice through collaborative research and evaluation. In addition, partners identified tobacco use as the top research priority for the PRC. These decisions became pivotal for the newly established Center and began a 15-year history of academic-state partnerships in tobacco control.

Action Steps

Several critical actions were taken. First, in 1995, West Virginia had the highest rate of teen smoking in the nation, and thus the academic-state partners determined that smoking cessation among teens would be the focus of the Center's core research project. Second, faculty were hired to work specifically on state-driven initiatives in tobacco research. Third, PRC funds were set aside to conduct tobacco-related pilot research using community-based participatory approaches. Fourth, state partners invited Center faculty to tobacco control meetings; the faculty were encouraged to provide guidance and research leadership. Partners also committed to ongoing collaborations through frequent conference calls, the sharing of resources, and using research to improve tobacco control policy and practice. In addition, a statewide focus for the PRC was reiterated. In 2001, the PRC formed and funded a statewide Community Partnership Board to ensure adequate representation and voice from across the state. This board provided input into the PRC's tobacco research agenda. Partners collectively framed pilot research on tobacco and the original core research project, the development and evaluation of the N-O-T teen smoking cessation program.

Significantly, the Bureau for Public Health, the Department of Education Office of Healthy Schools, and the PRC combined their resources to develop and evaluate N-O-T. Soon after, the American Lung Association (ALA) learned about N-O-T and was added as a partner. The ALA adopted N-O-T, and the program is now a federally designated model program with more than 10 years of research behind it. It is also the most widely used teen smoking cessation program in both the state and the nation (Dino et al., 2008). The Bureau's Division of Tobacco Prevention continues to provide resources to disseminate N-O-T statewide. The PRC, in turn, commits core funds to the Division's partnership activities.

Additionally, the PRC and the Office of Healthy Schools collaborated to assess West Virginia's use of the 1994 CDC-recommended guidelines on tobacco control policy and practice in schools. Partners codeveloped a statewide principals' survey and used survey data to create a new statewide school tobacco policy consistent with CDC guidelines (Tompkins et al., 1999). Within a year, the West Virginia Board of Education Tobacco-Free Schools Policy was established by Legislative Rule §126CSR66. As collaborations grew, the state received funds from the 2001 Master Settlement Agreement; some of these funds were used by the Division of Tobacco Prevention to establish an evaluation unit within the PRC. This unit became the evaluator for tobacco control projects funded through the Master Settlement as well as by other sources. The evaluation unit has been instrumental in helping the programs improve their process of awarding grants by helping to develop a request for proposals (RFP) and by providing training in grant writing and evaluation

Partners also committed to ongoing collaborations through frequent conference calls, the sharing of resources, and using research to improve tobacco control policy and practice.

to those applying for funds. The evaluators continue to develop tools and reporting guidelines to measure success. Through the years, this process has allowed the Division of Tobacco Prevention to identify the organizations best suited to carry out tobacco control efforts, and two highly successful, regional tobacco-focused networks have been created — one community based and the other school based. The Division, which consistently makes programmatic decisions based on evaluation reports and recommendations from the PRC, believes that the PRC-state collaboration has been one of the key partnerships leading to the many successes of the tobacco prevention and control program. In the words of Bruce Adkins, Director of the Division of Tobacco Prevention, the state-PRC evaluation partnerships:

> ensure that our tobacco prevention and cessation efforts are founded in science, responsive to communities, and accountable to state policy-makers. Based on PRC guidance and CDC Best Practices collaboration, we only fund evidence-based programs, and we continuously quantify and qualify every intervention we fund. Without the PRC, our division would have far fewer successes to share with the nation. (personal communication with Mr. Adkins, September 2008)

Take-Home Messages

- There must be an ongoing commitment to the partnership, and it must be reinforced on a continuing basis.

- Partners need to establish a set of shared values, such as recognizing the importance of a statewide focus, using CBPR approaches, and emphasizing the importance of research translation.

- Partners must commit to shared decision making and shared resources.

- Roles and responsibilities should be defined based on complementary skill sets.

- Partners must establish mutual respect and trust.

References

Dino G, Horn K, Abdulkadri A, Kalsekar I, Branstetter S. Cost-effectiveness analysis of the Not On Tobacco program for adolescent smoking cessation. *Prevention Science* 2008;9(1):38-46.

Tompkins NO, Dino GA, Zedosky LK, Harman M, Shaler G. A collaborative partnership to enhance school-based tobacco control policies in West Virginia. *American Journal of Preventive Medicine* 1999;16(3 Suppl):29-34.

Trust for America's Health. *West Virginia state data.* Washington (DC): Trust for America's Health; 2008.

4. INITIATING A PROJECT WITH A COMMUNITY AND DEVELOPING A COMMUNITY ADVISORY BOARD

As described in Chapter 1, partnerships evolve over time. Often, the first steps toward engagement are the most difficult to take. The vignettes in this section demonstrate some effective ways of initiating research collaborations.

A. How do you start working with a community?

Daniel S. Blumenthal, MD, MPH

Challenge

In the mid-1980s, the Morehouse School of Medicine in Atlanta was a new institution, having been founded only a few years earlier. Because its mission called for service to underserved communities, two contiguous low-income African American neighborhoods in southeast Atlanta were engaged. These neighborhoods, Joyland and Highpoint, had a combined population of about 5,000 and no established community organization. Morehouse dispatched a community organizer to the area, and he spent the next few months learning about the community. He met the community leaders, ministers, business-people, school principals, and agency heads, and he secured credibility by supporting neighborhood events and even buying t-shirts for a kids' softball team. Soon, he was able to bring together the leaders, who now knew and trusted him (and, by extension, Morehouse), to create and incorporate the Joyland-Highpoint Community Coalition (JHCC).

With the help of the community organizer, the JHCC conducted an assessment of the community's health needs, mostly by surveying people where they gathered and worked. Drug abuse was at the top of the community's problem list, and Morehouse secured a grant to conduct a project on preventing substance abuse. Most of the grant was subcontracted to the JHCC, which was able to use the funds to hire a project director (who also served as the organization's executive director) and other staff.

Action Steps

Morehouse continued to work with Joyland, Highpoint, and the surrounding neighborhoods (known collectively as "Neighborhood Planning Unit Y," or NPU-Y) for the next few years, even long after the original grant had expired. In the mid-1990s, it took advantage of the opportunity to apply to CDC for funds to establish a PRC. Applicants were required to have a community partner, and so Morehouse and NPU-Y became applicant partners. The grant was funded, and a community-majority board was created to govern the center. There were still issues to be worked out between the medical school and the community, such as the location of the center and the details of research protocols, but the foundation of trust allowed these issues to be resolved while preserving the partnership (Blumenthal, 2006).

Take-Home Messages

- Community partnerships are not built overnight. A trusting partnership is developed over months or years.

- A partnership does not depend on a single grant, or even a succession of grants. The partnership continues even when there are no grants.

- A partnership means that resources and control are shared. The academic institution or government agency must be prepared to share funds with the community. The community should be the "senior partner" on issues that affect it.

- Community representatives should primarily be people who live in the community. The programs and projects implemented by agencies, schools, and other entities affect the community, but their staff often live elsewhere.

Reference

Blumenthal DS. A community coalition board creates a set of values for community-based research. *Preventing Chronic Disease* 2006;3(1):A16.

B. How do you set up and maintain a community advisory board?

Tabia Henry Akintobi, PhD, MPH, Lisa Goodin, MBA, Ella H. Trammel, David Collins, Daniel S. Blumenthal, MD, MPH

Establishing a governing body that ensures community-engaged research is challenging when (1) academicians have not previously been guided by neighborhood experts in the evolution of a community's ecology, (2) community members have not led discussions regarding their health priorities, or (3) academic and neighborhood experts have not historically worked together as a single body with established rules to guide roles and operations. The Morehouse School of Medicine PRC was based on the applied definition of CBPR, in which research is conducted with, not on, communities in a partnership relationship. Faced with high levels of poverty, a lack of neighborhood resources, a plague of chronic diseases, and basic distrust in the research process, community members initially expressed their apprehension about participating in yet another partnership with an academic institution to conduct what they perceived as meaningless research in their neighborhoods.

Action Steps

Central to establishing the Morehouse Community Coalition Board (CCB) was an iterative process of disagreement, dialogue, and compromise that ultimately resulted in the identification of what academicians needed from neighborhood board members and what they, in turn, would offer communities. Not unlike other new social exchanges, each partner had to first learn, respect, and then value what the other considered a worthy benefit in return for participating on the CCB. According to the current CCB chair, community members allow researchers conditional access to their communities to engage in research with an established community benefit. Benefits to CCB members include the research findings as well as education, the building of skills and capacity, and an increased ability to access and navigate clinical and social services. The community has participated in Morehouse School of Medicine PRC CBPR focused on reducing the risk of HIV/AIDS and screening for colorectal cancer. Further, community-based radio broadcasts have facilitated real-time dialogue between metropolitan Atlanta community members and researchers to increase awareness regarding health promotion activities and various ways that communities can be empowered to improve their health. Other benefits have been the creation or expansion of jobs and health promotion programs through grants for community-led health initiatives.

Critical to maintaining the CCB are established bylaws that provide a blueprint for the governing body. As much as possible, board members should be people who truly represent the community and its priorities. Agency staff (e.g., health department staff, school principals) may not live in the community where they work, and so they may not be good representatives, even though their input has value. In the case of the Morehouse PRC, agency staff are included on the board, but residents of the community are in the majority, and one always serves as the CCB chair. All projects and protocols to be implemented by the PRC must be approved by the CCB's Project Review Committee, which consists of neighborhood representatives. For more than a decade, critical research has been implemented and communities have sustained change. The differing values of academic and community CCB representatives are acknowledged and coexist within an established infrastructure that supports collective functioning to address community health promotion initiatives (Blumenthal, 2006; Hatch et al., 1993).

> For more than a decade, critical research has been implemented and communities have sustained change.

Take-Home Messages

- Engagement in effective community coalition boards is developed through multi-directional learning of each partner's values and needs.

- Community coalition boards are built and sustained over time to ensure community ownership through established rules and governance structures.

- Trust and relationship building are both central to having neighborhood and research experts work together to shape community-engaged research agendas.

- Maintaining a community coalition board requires ongoing communication and feedback, beyond formal monthly or quarterly meetings, to keep members engaged.

References

Blumenthal DS. A community coalition board creates a set of values for community-based research. *Preventing Chronic Disease* 2006;3(1):A16.

Hatch J, Moss N, Saran A, Presley-Cantrell L, Mallory C. Community research: partnership in black communities. *American Journal of Preventive Medicine* 1993;9(6 Suppl):27-31.

C. How do you launch a major community-engaged research study with a brand-new partnership that brings together diverse entities and individuals?

Mina Silberberg, PhD, Sherman A. James, PhD, Elaine Hart-Brothers, MD, MPH, Seronda A. Robinson, PhD, Sharon Elliott-Bynum, PhD, RN

Challenge

As described in an earlier vignette, the African-American Health Improvement Partnership was launched in October 2005 in Durham, North Carolina, with a grant from the National Center for Minority Health and Health Disparities. AAHIP built on the prior work of participant organizations and individuals, but it created new relationships and was a new entity. The lead applicant on the grant was the Duke Division of Community Health (DCH), which had been working with community partners for seven years to develop innovative programs in care management, clinical services, and health education to meet the needs of underserved populations, primarily in Durham.

Until that point, research in the DCH had been limited to evaluation of its own programs, although some faculty and staff had conducted other types of research in their earlier positions. The AAHIP research team included Elaine Hart-Brothers, head of the Community Health Coalition (CHC), a community-based organization dedicated to addressing health disparities by mobilizing the volunteer efforts of Durham African American health professionals. The DCH had just begun working with the CHC through a small subcontract. Because the AAHIP was an entirely new entity, it had no community advisory board (CAB), and although the DCH and other Duke and Durham entities were engaged in collaborative work, no preexisting coalitions or advisory panels had the scope and composition required to support the AAHIP's proposed work.

Action Steps

The CHC was brought into the development of the grant proposal at the beginning, before the budget was developed, and it played a particularly important role in developing the CAB. The goal was to create a board that represented diverse sectors of Durham's African American and provider communities. On this issue, Sherman A. James (the study PI) and Mina Silberberg (currently the co-PI) deferred to the expertise of Hart-Brothers and Susan Yaggy, chief of the DCH, both of whom had broad and deep ties to the Durham community and years of experience with collaborative initiatives.

The research team decided it would be essential to evaluate its collaboration with the CAB to ensure fidelity to the principles of collaboration, to build capacity, and to help with the dissemination of lessons learned. For this external evaluation, it turned to North Carolina Central University (NCCU), enlisting the services of LaVerne Reid.

When the grant was awarded, it was time to bring together these diverse players and begin work in earnest. Hart-Brothers quickly realized that as a full-time community physician, she could not by herself fulfill CHC's role on the project: to serve as the community "outreach" arm of the research team and participate actively in study design, data collection and analysis, and dissemination. She proposed a budget reallocation to bring on Sharon Elliott-Bynum, a nurse and community activist with a long and distinguished history of serving Durham's low-income community. DCH faculty realized with time that Elliott-Bynum brought to the project unique expertise and contacts in sectors where DCH's own expertise and contacts were limited, particularly the African American faith community. Similarly, Reid, who had recently been appointed interim Associate Dean of the College of Behavioral and Social Sciences at NCCU, recognized that she no longer had the time to evaluate the CAB-research team collaboration on her own and brought in Seronda Robinson from NCCU.

As the work progressed, new challenges arose in the relationship between Duke and the CHC. As a small community-based organization, the CHC used accounting methods that did not meet Duke's requirements or those of NIH; invoices lacked sufficient detail and documentation. Payment to the CHC fell behind, as the DCH returned invoices it had received for revision, and both parties grew frustrated. The partners decided that the DCH administrator would develop written instructions for the CHC on invoicing for purposes of the grant and train CHC staff on these procedures. Eventually, CHC also brought on a staffer with greater skills in the accounting area.

Duke's lengthy process for payment of invoices frustrated the CHC, which, as a small organization, was unable to pay staff without a timely flow of funds. In response, the research team established that the CHC would tell the DCH immediately if its check did not arrive when expected, and the DCH would immediately check on payment status with the central accounting office. Moreover, the DCH determined that when the CHC needed a rapid influx of funds, it should invoice more frequently than once per month. In this way, through sustained engagement by all parties, the DCH and CHC moved from pointing fingers at each other to solving what had been a frustrating problem. In explaining the AAHIP's capacity to work through these invoicing issues, participants cite not only the actions taken in that moment but also a history of open communication and respect, particularly the inclusion of the CHC in the original budget and the understanding that all members of the research team are equal partners.

Take-Home Messages

- Create the preconditions for solving problems and conflicts through a history and environment of inclusion (particularly with regard to money).

- Recognize and use the unique expertise, skills, and connections of each partner. Step back when necessary to defer to others.

- Be flexible. The study needs will change, as will the circumstances of individual partners.

- Put the right people with the right level of commitment in the right job.

- Commit the staff time required for effective, active community participation on a research team.

- Communicate and invest in capacity building. The operating procedures and needs of academic institutions, federal agencies, and small community-based organizations are usually very different. As a result, community and academic partners may come to view each other, perhaps mistakenly, as uncooperative. Partners will need to learn each other's procedures and needs and then solve problems together. Community partners are also likely to need capacity building in the accounting procedures required by academic institutions and the federal government.

5. OVERCOMING COMPETING PRIORITIES AND INSTITUTIONAL DIFFERENCES

From the concepts of community set forth in Chapter 1 it is apparent that universities can be seen as communities that have their own norms, social networks, and functional sectors. How can we resolve the conflicts and misunderstandings that result when the operations and expectations of universities differ from those of their collaborating communities?

A. How do you work with a community when there are competing priorities and different expectations?

Karen Williams, PhD, John M. Cooks, Elizabeth Reifsnider, PhD, Sally B. Coleman

Challenge

A major priority for the University of Texas Medical Branch at Galveston when developing its CTSA proposal was to demonstrate community partnership with a viable, grassroots community-based organization (CBO). One of the coinvestigators listed on the CTSA proposal was a research affiliate of an active CBO, which was composed of persons representing practically every facet of life in the community. While focusing on its own organizational development, this CBO had identified eight community health needs for its focus and implemented two NIH-funded projects (Reifsnider et al., 2010). The CTSA coinvestigator wanted the CBO to be the community partner for the CTSA proposal, and the other CTSA investigators agreed. The brunt of the active work in the community outlined in the CTSA proposal became the CBO's responsibility. However, although the CTSA work was within the existing scope of work for the community partner, certain invalid assumptions about the type of activities the CBO would do for the CTSA were written into the final version of the grant. Most important, no budget was presented to the CBO that showed support for expected deliverables.

The CBO was unwilling to commit to being a part of the CTSA until the proposal spelled out in detail what it was required to do for the funds. An official meeting took place between selected CBO members and CTSA investigators; after an informal discussion, CBO members gave the university members a letter requesting specific items in return for their participation. A formal response to the letter was not provided by the university partner; instead, the requested changes were inserted into the proposal and a revised draft circulated to community partners with the assumption that it would address their requests. This was not the understanding of the community partners, and this misunderstanding strained future relationships. The CBO felt that it had not received the answers it had requested, and the university coinvestigator believed that revising the proposal addressed the CBO's requests. The miscommunication persisted for months and resulted in difficulty in establishing the operations of the CTSA once it was funded.

Action Steps

The issue was finally addressed when the university coinvestigator approached the CBO for help in writing another NIH proposal. At that time, it emerged that the CTSA-related issues had never been resolved and that the CBO felt its cooperation was being taken for granted. A meeting was held with the CBO president, another member, and two university researchers who were dues-paying members of the CBO. During this meeting, the misunderstanding was clarified and apologies were offered and accepted. Both the CBO and the university members realized that in a rush to complete grant-writing assignments, shortcuts had been taken that should have been avoided.

Take-Home Messages

- University partners should be clear in responding to written requests from a community for communication about specifics on research collaboration. Communications can be easily misunderstood by well-intentioned individuals. Asking for feedback should be routine practice.

- It is critical for partners to respect and include the input of the community they are trying to serve.

- The lines of communication must remain open until all issues are considered resolved by everyone involved.

- Transparency is always essential for all entities.

Reference

Reifsnider E, Hargraves M, Williams KJ, Cooks J, Hall V. Shaking and rattling: developing a child obesity prevention program using a faith-based community approach. *Family and Community Health* 2010;33(2):144-151.

B. How do you overcome differences in financial practices between the academic institution and the community?

Karen Williams, PhD, Sally B. Coleman, John M. Cooks, Elizabeth Reifsnider, PhD

Challenge

Academic research institutions and community organizations often partner on research projects even though they may differ significantly in key ways, including organizational capacity and the types of knowledge considered useful for social problem solving (Williams, 2009). Although evaluation tools exist for assessment of organizational capacity and for setting priorities (Butterfoss, 2007), tools for assessing the "fit" between partnering organizations are scarce. This vignette describes the challenges faced by a CBPR partnership during the preparation and implementation of a joint grant proposal.

> Academic research institutions and community organizations often partner on research projects even though they may differ significantly in key ways…

In October 2007, NIH announced the NIH Partners in Research Program. Each application was required to represent a partnership between the community and scientific investigators. Upon award, the grants were to be split into two separate but administratively linked awards. A community health coalition and university health science center that had worked together for several years submitted a joint proposal. Preparing the budget for the joint proposal highlighted power imbalances in the community-academic partnership. The university-based investigators' salaries were large relative to the salary of the community-based PI, which was based on what he earned as an elementary school music teacher. To direct more funds to the community partner, the partnership minimized the university-based investigators' time on the project and allocated all non-salary research funds to the budget of the community partner. This resulted in a

30% community/70% university split of direct costs. In addition, every dollar of direct cost awarded to the university partner garnered an additional 51 cents, because the university had negotiated a 51% indirect cost rate with NIH. However, the community partner received no indirect cost add-on because it had no negotiated rate with NIH. The irony in allocating program funding to the community partner was that this sharing gave the community partner more administrative work to do, even though the partner received no support from indirect costs.

A second challenge arose that highlighted the difference in expectations between university and community partners. The grant required that community workers facilitate discussion groups. To accomplish this, the community portion of the budget had to pay to train community workers and trainees as well as cover costs such as meeting rooms, food, and materials. Inevitably, the community's small pool of funds was exhausted, and some university funds were required. Getting community researchers and research expenses paid by the university took a month or longer. University faculty are accustomed to lengthy delays in reimbursement, but community members expect prompt payments. Both the community-based and university-based PIs were put in the uncomfortable position of having to continually ask those waiting for payment to be patient. Documentation procedures were not as extensive and wait times were shorter when community research funds flowed through the community organization.

A second challenge arose that highlighted the difference in expectations between university and community partners.

Action Steps

It would have been administratively easier for the university partner to pay the community partner on a subcontract. However, this arrangement was prohibited by NIH because the purpose of the Partners in Research grant was to establish an equal partnership. In future CBPR projects, the community partner may consider subcontracting as a way to decrease administrative burden, even if it decreases control over research funds. Also, the university-based PI should have more thoroughly investigated the procedures for university payments, alerted community members to the extended wait times for payments, and advocated for streamlined procedures with university administration and accounting.

Take-Home Messages

- "Splitting budgets in half" is too blunt a tool for the delicate work of building equal partnerships. Exploring more nuanced mechanisms to balance power between community and academic partners is critical.

- Make no assumptions about the capabilities of the institution (university or CBO) or how it functions.

- University and CBO partners need to come to agreement on all processes and timetables that might be involved.

- Foster open communication with those affected to maintain organizational and personal credibility.

References

Butterfoss FD. *Coalitions and partnerships in community health.* San Francisco: Jossey-Bass; 2007.

Williams KJ, Gail BP, Shapiro-Mendoza CK, Reisz I, Peranteau J. Modeling the principles of community-based participatory research in a community health assessment conducted by a health foundation. *Health Promotion Practice* 2009;10(1):67-75.

C. How do you harness the power and knowledge of multiple academic medical institutions and community partners?

Carolyn Leung Rubin, EdD, MA, Doug Brugge, PhD, MS, Jocelyn Chu, ScD, MPH, Karen Hacker, MD, MPH, Jennifer Opp, Alex Pirie, Linda Sprague Martinez, MA, Laurel Leslie, MD, MPH

Challenge

In some cases, several CTSA sites are clustered in a small geographic area and thus may be well suited to demonstrating how institutions can overcome competitive differences and work together for the good of their mutual communities.

In the Boston metropolitan area, three CTSA sites, Tufts University, Harvard University, and Boston University, prioritized working with each other and with community partners.

Action Steps

To facilitate their collaboration, the three sites took advantage of the CTSA program's Community Engagement Consultative Service, bringing two consultants to Boston to share insights about forming institutional partnerships in an urban area. Bernadette Boden-Albala from Columbia University in New York City and Jen Kauper-Brown from Northwestern University in Evanston, Illinois, visited Boston on separate occasions and shared their experiences in bringing together CTSA sites and community partners in their areas.

These visits helped to facilitate conversation among the three CTSAs about how to work together for the mutual benefit of the community. At the same time, the CTSAs each were having conversations with their community partners about the need to build capacity for research in the community. When a funding opportunity arose through the American Recovery and Reinvestment Act of 2009, the three CTSAs, along with two critical community partners, the Center for Community Health Education Research and Services and the Immigrant Services Providers Group/Health, decided to collaboratively develop a training program to build research capacity.

Of the 35 organizations that applied for the first round of funding, 10 were selected in January 2010 to make up the first cohort of community research fellows. These fellows underwent a five-month training course that included such topics as policy, ethics, research design, the formulation of questions, and methods. The community organizations represented in the training varied in size, geographic location, and the types of "communities" served (e.g., disease-specific advocacy organizations, immigration groups, and public housing advocacy groups specific to certain geographic boundaries). The program used a "community-centered" approach in its design, feedback about each session was rapidly cycled back into future sessions, and learning was shared between community and academic researchers. The first cohort concluded its work in 2010. Outcomes and insights from the project will feed the next round of training.

Although the CTSA sites in the Boston area were already committed to working together, bringing in consultants with experience in working across academic institutions helped them think through a process and learn from other regions' experiences. The consultants affirmed that, by working together, academic medical centers can better serve the needs of their mutual community rather than the individual needs of the institutions. This was echoed by participants in the capacity-building program described above. One clear response from participants was their appreciation that the three academic institutions partnered to work with communities rather than splintering their efforts and asking community groups to align with one institution or another.

Take-Home Messages

- Research training programs need to model multidirectional knowledge exchange; the knowledge of community members must be valued and embedded into the curriculum alongside academic knowledge.

- Transparency, honesty, and sharing of resources (fiscal and human) among academic institutions and community groups are crucial to building trust.

- Academic institutions can and should work together on the common mission of serving their communities. Outside consultants can help facilitate multi-institutional collaboration.

CONCLUSION

The vignettes presented here illustrate key challenges in CEnR and provide examples of how partnerships have dealt with them. Ultimately, what underpins the solutions presented here are the same ideals encapsulated in the principles of community engagement — clarity of purpose, willingness to learn, time, understanding differences, building trust, communication, sharing of control, respect, capacity building, partnership, and commitment.

The Value of Social Networking in Community Engagement

Chapter 6
The Value of Social Networking in Community Engagement

Ann Dozier, PhD (Chair), Karen Hacker, MD, MPH, Mina Silberberg, PhD, Linda Ziegahn, PhD

INTRODUCTION

Communities are not made up of unrelated individuals or groups; rather, they include "social networks" that comprise community groups or organizations, individuals, and the relations or "linkages" among them. Social networks are crucial to every aspect of community engagement, from understanding the community and its health issues to mobilizing the community for health improvement. A growing literature is highlighting the role that individuals' social networks play in conditioning their health, and the emergence of electronic social media provides new ways to form and engage networks. For these reasons, we devote an entire chapter to the role of social networks in community engagement, beginning with an overview of the topic and then moving to a focused look at the new social media.

WHAT ARE SOCIAL NETWORKS?

As defined by Wasserman et al. (1994), "A *social network* consists of a finite set of actors and the relation or relations defined on them" (p. 20). Any one individual can be part of multiple social networks, and the nature of these networks and the individual's connection to the networks can vary greatly. For example, social networks are not necessarily rooted in traditional relationships, such as kinship or clan, but can develop out of geographic proximity, work relationships, or recreational activities. Moreover, social networks can be described and analyzed in terms of their diverse characteristics (e.g., how many people or organizations belong to a network, how well the members of the network know each other, and how equal their relationships are).

SOCIAL NETWORKS AND HEALTH

Social networks can be a key factor in determining how healthy a community is. For one thing, they can create social supports that provide a buffer against the stressors that damage health (House et al., 1998; Zilberberg, 2011). Social networks may also have negative effects on health, however (Arthur, 2002; Cattell, 2001). Christakis et al. (2007), for example, found "clusters" of obesity within a network of people studied over time. Their longitudinal analysis suggested that these clusters were not merely the result of like-minded or similarly situated people forming ties with one another, but rather reflected the "spread" of obesity among people who were connected to each other (Christakis et al., 2007). Although not everyone agrees on how social networks affect health (Cohen-Cole et al., 2008), they seem to play a role, together with culture, economics, and other factors, that is important for both individuals and communities (Pachucki et al., 2010).

> Social networks can be a key factor in determining how healthy a community is.

In New York City, for example, one group tailored its outreach and education programs on breast and cervical cancer by determining how differing cultural perspectives affected social networks. They found that for the Latino population, women's relationships easily lent themselves to the helper role, but that access to and utilization of health care in this population were mediated by men. Therefore, they included both genders in their intervention (Erwin et al., 2007).

Social networks can also play an important part in community health improvement because of their role in the "diffusion of innovation" — a concept introduced in Chapter 1 — and in the generation of social capital, defined by Putnam (1995) as "features of social organization such as networks, norms, and social trust that facilitate coordination and cooperation for mutual benefit" (p. 66). A critical first step in engaging communities is identifying networks, such as faith communities, whose "social capital" can be employed in collective approaches to improving community health.

THE ROLE OF SOCIAL NETWORKS IN COMMUNITY ENGAGEMENT

Chapter 4 outlined four practice elements for development of a constituency (know the community, establish strategies, build networks, and mobilize communities) and used them to conceptualize the tasks of community engagement (Hatcher et al., 2008). In this chapter, we will use these four elements to describe the role and importance of social networks in community engagement.

Know Communities

Learning about a community, whether it is defined geographically or by a common interest (for example, a health condition or disease) means knowing the community's cultures and institutions, its capabilities and assets, and its health needs and challenges. Typically, learning about a community requires a variety of approaches, including gathering existing data and generating new information, combining qualitative and quantitative data, and incorporating the perspectives of a broad spectrum of individuals, organizations, and groups.

Understanding a community's social networks is essential because of their potential to affect population health. Social networks can also provide access to a community and generate knowledge of its characteristics. For example, traditional healers may be widely known within Hmong or Latino networks but unknown to those outside these social networks, including those working in health care institutions in the same community. It is only by bridging to the relevant networks that health care workers can learn about these traditional healers.

Social network analysis (SNA) is a method that can be used to evaluate community engagement and assess communities. By providing a way of describing the diversity of networks and a set of tools for visually representing and quantifying the characteristics of a network, SNA can help partners understand a community's networks and track how they grow and change over time. This methodology is discussed further in Chapter 7.

Establish Positions and Strategies

Social networks represent important groups of constituents in any community health planning initiative. These groups can be engaged to provide feedback, identify priorities and opportunities, establish positions on issues and approaches, and plan strategies for intervention. Both obtaining knowledge *about* social networks and gathering knowledge *from* such networks are essential to the development of relevant strategies for health improvement. In addition, social networks are a means of communication, creating a platform for sharing and discussing potential positions and strategies.

Build and Sustain Networks

Building and sustaining networks of individuals and entities for community health improvement or research includes establishing and maintaining communication channels, exchanging resources, and coordinating collaborative activities. Existing social networks can be effective and efficient platforms for efforts in community engagement if they reach people who are central to these efforts and if their members share the goals of the engagement efforts. Through the community engagement process, new networks can be developed as well.

Mobilize Constituencies

Ultimately, partners and their constituencies must be mobilized to take the actions that will lead to improved community health, and mobilization must be sustained through leadership, communication, and motivation. As described earlier in this chapter, this is where the social capital embedded in social networks is of the utmost importance. Throughout the community engagement effort, relationships must be strengthened and new capacity for collective action developed. It is important to reach out and pull in key opinion leaders and community stakeholders.

In one example of how this can work, a clinician-researcher at the University of California, Davis, used social networks to help reduce dog bites among children. After noticing that a large number of children were being seen for treatment of dog bites, the investigator identified social networks such as dog owners, school crossing guards, and neighborhood associations and engaged them in understanding the problem, defining workable solutions, and mobilizing the community to put these solutions into action (Pan et al., 2005).

ELECTRONIC SOCIAL MEDIA AND COMMUNITY ENGAGEMENT

Introduction

The tools of electronic social media, such as Facebook and Twitter, can be used to track, support, create, and mobilize social networks; these tools have significant potential to enhance community engagement efforts (Fine, 2006). Social media venues have undergone a significant shift to greater bidirectional or multidirectional communication in recent years (Bacon, 2009), and thus these venues represent opportunities for health messaging that have yet to be fully realized. In addition, they provide new forums to raise issues, facilitate the exchange of ideas, and engage a larger community.

The Potential of Social Media

Social media tools provide a newly emerging mechanism for engaging a large and diverse group of participants, including individuals or groups that might otherwise be hard to reach or to bring together, such as individuals with a rare disease (Bacon, 2009; Fine, 2006). Social media also provide a forum for discussion that has important differences from face-to-face interactions. With social media, all participants have an opportunity to contribute to the discussion, responses need not be immediate, and time can be taken to review the thread of a discussion. Social media also provide opportunities to reframe questions as the discussion evolves (Connor, 2009).

In addition, social media can generate a discussion archive that is useful for revisiting opinions, information, and collective history. Furthermore, the manner in which social media are used by the community in the initial stages of engagement might be a barometer of the capacity to engage that community and success in doing so, facilitating evaluation of community engagement.

Generally, depending on how groups communicate, a broader group of participants can be engaged using social media than through traditional means, facilitating the process of establishing collective positions and strategies. Specifically, social media can provide a forum for interaction and discussion about both draft and final position statements. Clearly, social media also play an important role in building and sustaining networks by facilitating ongoing communication, social exchange, and coordination of activities. Moreover, these media can help build trust by providing venues in which partners can demonstrate transparency and openness. Meeting agendas, minutes, handouts, and questions (and responses) can all be posted and viewed.

Finally, social media can be a tool for mobilizing organizations and community members and, even more important, social media can help sustain engagement and commitment. Social media can also offer accessible sites to provide information about a developing engagement, such as its purpose and goals and who is involved (Bacon, 2009; Connor, 2009).

Cautions on the Use of Social Media

Many of the cautions about social media are similar to those for any community engagement activity (Bacon, 2009). For example, when appraising face-to-face interactions, we ask, are the responses honest? Will people have the time to participate? We need to ask those questions about the use of social media, too. However, use of social media raises additional concerns about who is actually participating and whether they are who they represent themselves to be. Building trust is essential for community engagement, and networking through social media alone is unlikely to achieve the level of trust needed for collective action. Rather than being seen as a substitute for in-person interactions, social media may be better viewed as supplementary or complementary, particularly in the early stages of community engagement. Furthermore, social media should not be regarded as an inexpensive alternative to the in-person building of relationships. Like any community engagement effort, use of social media for communication engagement will take time (Connor, 2009). Overall, it is important to understand the modes of communication employed by the community of interest and then use those modes.

Time is a particular concern for the person who plays the crucial role of moderating a social media forum. It is the moderator's job to demonstrate that someone is listening, keep the discussion developing, and recruit and retain members. There are many ways in which an online community can be undermined, and it is the moderator's job to enforce the "rules of engagement." Once established, a forum requires regular attention. Given the pace of interactions in the social media environment, moderating a forum may require visiting the site several times a day (Bacon, 2009).

Recommendations about specific products have not been included in this chapter, because products continue to evolve. Furthermore, although the discussion addresses how social media can be used, the question of whether or when it is appropriate to use specific social media is contingent upon the nature of the individual project, available resources, and the appropriateness of the tool for the particular community. Given the resources necessary to involve social media, it would be a mistake to try to be "everywhere." Engagement is an iterative process; organizations should be selective, determine which media (if any) the community of interest are already using, and ask the community what approaches (if any) should be used and at what time in the engagement process social media should be introduced. Like all decisions about community engagement strategies, decisions about the use of social media should be made by engaging the community.

Given the resources necessary to involve social media, it would be a mistake to try to be "everywhere."

CONCLUSION

Social networks are an important tool for understanding a community and mobilizing it for health improvement. New research literature has brought increased attention to the role that social networks can play in population health, and the growing use of community-engaged health promotion and research has brought to the fore the potential for social networks to support collective action for health improvement. Moreover, the emergence of electronic social media has diversified the ways in which networks can be formed and engaged. "Networking," whether in person or electronically, is not the same as creating, sustaining, or engaging a community; if done incorrectly, it can undermine rather than support collaborative efforts. The principles laid out in this primer must be applied to the use of social networks just as they should be to all engagement efforts.

REFERENCES

Arthur T. The role of social networks: a novel hypothesis to explain the phenomenon of racial disparity in kidney transplantation. *American Journal of Kidney Diseases* 2002;40(4):678-681.

Bacon J. *The art of community: building the new age of participation (theory in practice).* Sebastopol (CA): O'Reilly Media; 2009.

Cattell V. Poor people, poor places, and poor health: the mediating role of social networks and social capital. *Social Science and Medicine* 2001;52:1501-1516.

Christakis NA, Fowler JH. The spread of obesity in a large social network over 32 years. *New England Journal of Medicine* 2007;357(4):370-379.

Cohen-Cole E, Fletcher JM. Detecting implausible social network effects in acne, height, and headaches: longitudinal analysis. *BMJ* 2008;337:a2533.

Connor A. *18 rules of community engagement: a guide for building relationships and connecting with customers online.* Silicon Valley (CA): Happy About; 2009.

Erwin DO, Johnson, VA, Trevino M, Duke K, Feliciano L, Jandorf L. A comparison of African American and Latina social networks as indicators for culturally tailoring a breast and cervical cancer education intervention. *Cancer* 2007;109(2 Suppl): 368-377.

Fine A. *Igniting social change and the connected age.* San Francisco: Jossey-Bass; 2006.

Hatcher MT, Nicola RM. Building constituencies for public health. In: Novick LF, Morrow CB, Mays GP (editors). *Public health administration: principles for population-based management* (2nd ed., pp. 443-458). Sudbury (MA): Jones and Bartlett; 2008.

House JS, Umberson D, Landis K. Structures and processes of social support. *Annual Review of Sociology* 1998;14:293-318.

Pachucki M, Breiger, R. Cultural holes: beyond relationality in social networks and culture. *Annual Review of Sociology* 2010;36:205-224.

Pan RJ, Littlefield D, Valladolid SG, Tapping PJ, West DC. Building healthier communities for children and families: applying asset-based community development to community pediatrics. *Pediatrics* 2005;115(4 Suppl):1185-1187.

Putnam RD. Bowling alone: America's declining social capital. *Journal of Democracy* 1995;6(1):65-78.

Wasserman S, Faust K. *Social network analysis: methods and applications.* Cambridge, United Kingdom: Cambridge University; 1994.

Zilberberg MD. The clinical research enterprise: time to change course? *JAMA* 2011;305(6):604-605.

Program Evaluation and Evaluating Community Engagement

Chapter 7
Program Evaluation and Evaluating Community Engagement

Meryl Sufian, PhD (Chair), Jo Anne Grunbaum, EdD (Co-Chair), Tabia Henry Akintobi, PhD, MPH, Ann Dozier, PhD, Milton (Mickey) Eder, PhD, Shantrice Jones, MPH, Patricia Mullan, PhD, Charlene Raye Weir, RN, PhD, Sharrice White-Cooper, MPH

BACKGROUND

A common theme through Chapters 1–6 was that community engagement develops over time and that its development is largely based on ongoing co-learning about how to enhance collaborations. The evaluation of community engagement programs provides an opportunity to assess and enhance these collaborations. Community members can be systematically engaged in assessing the quality of a community-engaged initiative, measuring its outcomes, and identifying opportunities for improvement.

This chapter summarizes the central concepts in program evaluation relevant to community engagement programs, including definitions, categories, approaches, and issues to anticipate. The chapter is not intended as a comprehensive overview of program evaluation; instead, the focus is on the importance of evaluating community-engaged initiatives and methods for this evaluation. With this in mind, Chapter 7 will present the following: (1) a definition of evaluation, (2) evaluation phases and processes, (3) two approaches to evaluation that are particularly relevant for the evaluation of community-engaged initiatives, (4) specific evaluation methods, and (5) challenges to be overcome to ensure an effective evaluation. Stakeholder engagement (i.e., inclusion of persons involved in or affected by programs) constitutes a major theme in the evaluation frameworks. In addition, methodological approaches and recommendations for communication and dissemination will be included. Examples are used throughout the chapter for illustrative purposes.

PROGRAM EVALUATION

Program evaluation can be defined as "the systematic collection of information about the activities, characteristics, and outcomes of programs, for use by people to reduce uncertainties, improve effectiveness, and make decisions" (Patton, 2008, p. 39). This utilization-focused definition guides us toward including the goals, concerns, and perspectives of program stakeholders. The results of evaluation are often used by stakeholders to improve or increase capacity of the program or activity. Furthermore, stakeholders can identify program priorities, what constitutes "success," and the data sources that could serve to answer questions about the acceptability, possible participation levels, and short- and long-term impact of proposed programs.

The community as a whole and individual community groups are both key stakeholders for the evaluation of a community engagement program. This type of evaluation needs to identify the relevant community and establish its perspectives so that the views of engagement leaders and all the important components of the community are used to identify areas for improvement. This approach includes determining whether the appropriate persons or organizations are involved; the activities they are involved in; whether participants feel they have significant input; and how engagement develops, matures, and is sustained.

Program evaluation uses the methods and design strategies of traditional research, but in contrast to the more inclusive, utility-focused approach of evaluation, research is a systematic investigation designed to develop or contribute to generalizable knowledge (MacDonald et al., 2001). Research is hypothesis driven, often initiated and controlled by an investigator, concerned with research standards of internal and external validity, and designed to generate facts, remain value-free, and focus on specific variables. Research establishes a time sequence and control for potential confounding variables. Often, the research is widely disseminated. Evaluation, in contrast, may or may not contribute to generalizable knowledge. The primary purposes of an evaluation are to assess the processes and outcomes of a specific initiative and to facilitate ongoing program management. Evaluation of a program usually includes multiple measures that are informed by the contributions and perspectives of diverse stakeholders.

Evaluation can be classified into five types by intended use: formative, process, summative, outcome, and impact. Formative evaluation provides information to guide program improvement, whereas process evaluation determines whether a program is delivered as intended to the targeted recipients (Rossi et al., 2004). Formative and process evaluations are appropriate to conduct during the implementation of a program. Summative evaluation informs judgments about whether the program worked (i.e., whether the goals and objectives were met) and requires making explicit the criteria and evidence being used to make "summary" judgments. Outcome evaluation focuses on the observable conditions of a specific population, organizational attribute, or social condition that a program is expected to have changed. Whereas outcome evaluation tends to focus on conditions or behaviors that the program was expected to affect most directly and immediately (i.e., "proximal" outcomes), impact evaluation examines the program's long-term goals. Summative, outcome, and impact evaluation are appropriate to conduct when the program either has been completed or has been ongoing for a substantial period of time (Rossi et al., 2004).

> Evaluation can be classified into five types by intended use: formative, process, summative, outcome, and impact.

For example, assessing the strategies used to implement a smoking cessation program and determining the degree to which it reached the target population are process evaluations. In contrast, an outcome evaluation of a smoking cessation program might examine how many of the program's participants stopped smoking as compared with persons who did not participate. Reduction in morbidity and mortality associated with cardiovascular disease may represent an impact goal for a smoking cessation program (Rossi et al., 2004).

Several institutions have identified guidelines for an effective evaluation. For example, in 1999, CDC published a framework to guide public health professionals in developing and implementing a program evaluation (CDC, 1999). The impetus for the framework was to facilitate the integration of evaluation into public health programs, but the framework focuses on six components that are critical for any evaluation. Although the components are interdependent and might be implemented in a nonlinear order, the earlier domains provide a foundation for subsequent areas. They include:

- Engage stakeholders to ensure that all partners invested in what will be learned from the evaluation become engaged early in the evaluation process.

- Describe the program to clearly identify its goals and objectives. This description should include the program's needs, expected outcomes, activities, resources, stage of development, context, and logic model.

- Design the evaluation design to be useful, feasible, ethical, and accurate.

- Gather credible evidence that strengthens the results of the evaluation and its recommendations. Sources of evidence could include people, documents, and observations.

- Justify conclusions that are linked to the results and judged against standards or values of the stakeholders.

- Deliberately ensure use of the evaluation and share lessons learned from it.

Five years before CDC issued its framework, the Joint Committee on Standards for Educational Evaluation (1994) created an important and practical resource for improving program evaluation. The Joint Committee, a nonprofit coalition of major professional organizations concerned with the quality of program evaluations, identified four major categories of standards — propriety, utility, feasibility, and accuracy — to consider when conducting a program evaluation.

Propriety standards focus on ensuring that an evaluation will be conducted legally, ethically, and with regard for promoting the welfare of those involved in or affected by the program evaluation. In addition to the rights of human subjects that are the concern of institutional review boards, propriety standards promote a service orientation (i.e., designing evaluations to address and serve the needs of the program's targeted participants), fairness in identifying program strengths and weaknesses, formal agreements, avoidance or disclosure of conflict of interest, and fiscal responsibility.

Utility standards are intended to ensure that the evaluation will meet the information needs of intended users. Involving stakeholders, using credible evaluation methods, asking pertinent questions, including stakeholder perspectives, and providing clear and timely evaluation reports represent attention to utility standards.

Feasibility standards are intended to make sure that the evaluation's scope and methods are realistic. The scope of the information collected should ensure that the data provide stakeholders with sufficient information to make decisions regarding the program.

Accuracy standards are intended to ensure that evaluation reports use valid methods for evaluation and are transparent in the description of those methods. Meeting accuracy standards might, for example, include using mixed methods (e.g., quantitative and qualitative), selecting justifiable informants, and drawing conclusions that are consistent with the data.

Together, the CDC framework and the Joint Committee standards provide a general perspective on the characteristics of an effective evaluation. Both identify the need to be pragmatic and serve intended users with the goal of determining the effectiveness of a program.

EVALUATION PHASES AND PROCESSES

The program evaluation process goes through four phases — planning, implementation, completion, and dissemination and reporting — that complement the phases of program development and implementation. Each phase has unique issues, methods, and procedures. In this section, each of the four phases is discussed.

Planning

The relevant questions during evaluation planning and implementation involve determining the feasibility of the evaluation, identifying stakeholders, and specifying short- and long-term goals. For example, does the program have the clarity of objectives or transparency in its methods required for evaluation? What criteria were used to determine the need for the program? Questions asked during evaluation planning also should consider the program's conceptual framework or underpinnings. For example, does a proposed community-engaged research program draw on "best practices" of other programs, including the characteristics of successful researcher-community partnerships? Is the program gathering information to ensure that it works in the current community context?

> Defining and identifying stakeholders is a significant component of the planning stage.

Defining and identifying stakeholders is a significant component of the planning stage. Stakeholders are people or organizations that have an interest in or could be affected by the program evaluation. They can be people who are involved in program operations, people who are served or affected by the program, or the primary users of the evaluation. The inclusion of stakeholders in an evaluation not only helps build support for the evaluation but also increases its credibility, provides a participatory approach, and supplies the multiple perspectives of participants and partners (Rossi et al., 2004).

Stakeholders might include community residents, businesses, community-based organizations, schools, policy makers, legislators, politicians, educators, researchers, media, and the public. For example, in the evaluation of a program to increase access to healthy food choices in and near schools, stakeholders could include store merchants, school boards, zoning commissions, parents, and students. Stakeholders constitute an important resource for identifying the questions a program evaluation should consider, selecting the methodology to be used, identifying data sources, interpreting findings, and implementing recommendations (CDC, 1999).

Once stakeholders are identified, a strategy must be created to engage them in all stages of the evaluation. Ideally, this engagement takes place from the beginning of the project or program or, at least, the beginning of the evaluation. The stakeholders should know that they are an important part of the evaluation and will be consulted on an ongoing basis throughout its development and implementation. The relationship between the stakeholders and the evaluators should involve two-way communication, and stakeholders should be comfortable initiating ideas and suggestions. One strategy to engage stakeholders in community programs and evaluations is to establish a community advisory board to oversee programs and evaluation activities in the community. This structure can be established as a resource to draw upon for multiple projects and activities that involve community engagement.

An important consideration when engaging stakeholders in an evaluation, beginning with its planning, is the need to understand and embrace cultural diversity. Recognizing diversity can improve the evaluation and ensure that important constructs and concepts are measured.

Implementation — Formative and Process Evaluation

Evaluation during a program's implementation may examine whether the program is successfully recruiting and retaining its intended participants, using training materials that meet standards for accuracy and clarity, maintaining its projected timelines, coordinating efficiently with other ongoing programs and activities, and meeting applicable legal standards. Evaluation during program implementation could be used to inform mid-course corrections to program implementation (formative evaluation) or to shed light on implementation processes (process evaluation).

For community-engaged initiatives, formative and process evaluation can include evaluation of the process by which partnerships are created and maintained and ultimately succeed in functioning.

Completion — Summative, Outcome, and Impact Evaluation

Following completion of the program, evaluation may examine its immediate outcomes or long-term impact or summarize its overall performance, including, for example, its efficiency and sustainability. A program's outcome can be defined as "the state of the target population or the social conditions that a program is expected to have changed," (Rossi et al., 2004, p. 204). For example, control of blood glucose was an appropriate program outcome when the efficacy of empowerment-based education of diabetes patients was evaluated (Anderson et al., 2009). In contrast, the number of people who received the empowerment education or any program service would not be considered a program outcome unless participation in and of itself represented a change in behavior or attitude (e.g., participating in a program to treat substance abuse). Similarly, the number of elderly housebound people receiving meals would not be considered a program outcome, but the nutritional benefits of the meals actually consumed for the health of the elderly, as well as improvements in their perceived quality of life, would be appropriate program outcomes (Rossi et al., 2004). Program evaluation also can determine the extent to which a change in an outcome can be attributed to the program. If a partnership is being evaluated, the contributions of that partnership to program outcomes may also be part of the evaluation. The CBPR model presented in Chapter 1 is an example of a model that could be used in evaluating both the process and outcomes of partnership.

> Once the positive outcome of a program is confirmed, subsequent program evaluation may examine the long-term impact the program hopes to have.

Once the positive outcome of a program is confirmed, subsequent program evaluation may examine the long-term impact the program hopes to have. For example, the outcome of a program designed to increase the skills and retention of health care workers in a medically underserved area would not be represented by the number of providers who participated in the training program, but it could be represented by the proportion of health care workers who stay for one year. Reduction in maternal mortality might constitute the long-term impact that such a program would hope to effect (Mullan, 2009).

Dissemination and Reporting

To ensure that the dissemination and reporting of results to all appropriate audiences is accomplished in a comprehensive and systematic manner, one needs to develop a dissemination plan during the planning stage of the evaluation. This plan should include guidelines on who will present results, which audiences will receive the results, and who will be included as a coauthor on manuscripts and presentations.

Dissemination of the results of the evaluation requires adequate resources, such as people, time, and money. Finding time to write papers and make presentations may be difficult for community members who have other commitments (Parker et al., 2005). In addition, academics may not be rewarded for nonscientific presentations and may thus be hesitant to spend time on such activities. Additional resources may be needed for the translation of materials to ensure that they are culturally appropriate.

Although the content and format of reporting may vary depending on the audience, the emphasis should be on full disclosure and a balanced assessment so that results can be used to strengthen the program. Dissemination of results may also be used for building capacity among stakeholders.

APPROACHES TO EVALUATION

Two approaches are particularly useful when framing an evaluation of community engagement programs; both engage stakeholders. In one, the emphasis is on the importance of participation; in the other, it is on empowerment. The first approach, participatory evaluation, actively engages the community in all stages of the evaluation process. The second approach, empowerment evaluation, helps to equip program personnel with the necessary skills to conduct their own evaluation and ensure that the program runs effectively. This section describes the purposes and characteristics of the two approaches.

Participatory Evaluation

Participatory evaluation can help improve program performance by (1) involving key stakeholders in evaluation design and decision making, (2) acknowledging and addressing asymmetrical levels of power and voice among stakeholders, (3) using multiple and varied methods, (4) having an action component so that evaluation findings are useful to the program's end users, and (5) explicitly aiming to build the evaluation capacity of stakeholders (Burke, 1998).

Characteristics of participatory evaluation include the following (Patton, 2008):

- The focus is on participant ownership; the evaluation is oriented to the needs of the program stakeholders rather than the funding agency.

- Participants meet to communicate and negotiate to reach a consensus on evaluation results, solve problems, and make plans to improve the program.

- Input is sought and recognized from all participants.

- The emphasis is on identifying lessons learned to help improve program implementation and determine whether targets were met.

- The evaluation design is flexible and determined (to the extent possible) during the group processes.

- The evaluation is based on empirical data to determine what happened and why.

- Stakeholders may conduct the evaluation with an outside expert serving as a facilitator.

Empowerment Evaluation

Empowerment evaluation is an approach to help ensure program success by providing stakeholders with tools and skills to evaluate their program and ensuring that the evaluation is part of the planning and management of the program (Fetterman, 2008). The major goal of empowerment evaluation is to transfer evaluation activities from an external evaluator to the stakeholders. Empowerment evaluation has four steps: (1) taking stock of the program and determining where it stands, including its strengths and weaknesses; (2) establishing goals for the future with an explicit emphasis on program improvement; (3) developing strategies to help participants determine their own strengths that they can use to accomplish program goals and activities; and (4) helping program participants decide on and gather the evidence needed to document progress toward achieving their goals (Fetterman, 1994).

> The major goal of empowerment evaluation is to transfer evaluation activities from an external evaluator to the stakeholders.

Characteristics of empowerment evaluation include the following (Wandersman et al., 2005):

- Values improvement in people, programs, and organizations to help them achieve results.

- Community ownership of the design and conduct of the evaluation and implementation of the findings.

- Inclusion of appropriate participants from all levels of the program, funders, and community.

- Democratic participation and clear and open evaluation plans and methods.

- Commitment to social justice and a fair allocation of resources, opportunities, obligations, and bargaining power.

- Use of community knowledge to understand the local context and to interpret results.

- Use of evidence-based strategies with adaptations to the local environment and culture.

- Building the capacity of program staff and participants to improve their ability to conduct their own evaluations.

- Organizational learning, ensuring that programs are responsive to changes and challenges.

- Accountability to funders' expectations.

Potential Disadvantages of Participatory and Empowerment Evaluation

The potential disadvantages of participatory and empowerment evaluation include (1) the possibility that the evaluation will be viewed as less objective because of stakeholder involvement, (2) difficulties in addressing highly technical aspects, (3) the need for time and resources when involving an array of stakeholders, and (4) domination and misuse by some stakeholders to further their own interests. However, the benefits of fully engaging stakeholders throughout the evaluation outweigh these concerns (Fetterman et al., 1996).

Table 7.1. Types of Evaluation Questions by Evaluation Phase

	TYPES OF EVALUATION QUESTIONS	
Evaluation Stage	**Quantitative**	**Qualitative**
Planning	What is the prevalence of the problem?	What are the values of the different stakeholders? What are the expectations and goals of participants?
Implementation	How many individuals are participating? What are the changes in performance? How many/what resources are used during implementation?	How are participants experiencing the change? How does the program change the way individuals relate to or feel about each other? To what extent is the intervention culturally and contextually valid?
Outcome	Is there a change in quality of life? Is there a change in biological and health measures? Is there a difference between those who were involved in the intervention and those who were not?	How has the culture changed? What themes underscore the participant's experience? What metaphors describe the change? What are the participant's personal stories? Were there any unanticipated benefits?

References: Holland et al., 2005; Steckler et al., 1992.

EVALUATION METHODS

An evaluation can use quantitative or qualitative data, and often includes both. Both methods provide important information for evaluation, and both can improve community engagement. These methods are rarely used alone; combined, they generally provide the best overview of the project. This section describes both quantitative and qualitative methods, and Table 7.1 shows examples of quantitative and qualitative questions according to stage of evaluation.

Quantitative Methods

Quantitative data provide information that can be counted to answer such questions as "How many?", "Who was involved?", "What were the outcomes?", and "How much did it cost?" Quantitative data can be collected by surveys or questionnaires, pretests and posttests, observation, or review of existing documents and databases or by gathering clinical data. Surveys may be self- or interviewer-administered and conducted face-to-face or by telephone, by mail, or online. Analysis of quantitative data involves statistical analysis, from basic descriptive statistics to complex analyses.

Quantitative data measure the depth and breadth of an implementation (e.g., the number of people who participated, the number of people who completed the program). Quantitative data collected before and after an intervention can show its outcomes and impact. The strengths of quantitative data for evaluation purposes include their generalizability (if the sample represents the population), the ease of analysis, and their consistency and precision (if collected reliably). The limitations of using quantitative data for evaluation can include poor response rates from surveys, difficulty obtaining documents, and difficulties in valid measurement. In addition, quantitative data do not provide an understanding of the program's context and may not be robust enough to explain complex issues or interactions (Holland et al., 2005; Garbarino et al., 2009).

Qualitative Methods

Qualitative data answer such questions as "What is the value added?", "Who was responsible?", and "When did something happen?" Qualitative data are collected through direct or participant observation, interviews, focus groups, and case studies and from written documents. Analyses of qualitative data include examining, comparing and contrasting, and interpreting patterns. Analysis will likely include the identification of themes, coding, clustering similar data, and reducing data to meaningful and important points, such as in grounded theory-building or other approaches to qualitative analysis (Patton, 2002).

Observations may help explain behaviors as well as social context and meanings because the evaluator sees what is actually happening. Observations can include watching a participant or program, videotaping an intervention, or even recording people who have been asked to "think aloud" while they work (Ericsson et al., 1993).

Interviews may be conducted with individuals alone or with groups of people and are especially useful for exploring complex issues. Interviews may be structured and conducted under controlled conditions, or they may be conducted with a loose set of questions asked in an open-ended manner. It may be helpful to tape-record interviews, with appropriate permissions, to facilitate the analysis of themes or content. Some interviews have a specific focus, such as a critical incident that an individual recalls and describes in detail. Another type of interview focuses on a person's perceptions and motivations.

Focus groups are run by a facilitator who leads a discussion among a group of people who have been chosen because they have specific characteristics (e.g., were clients of the program being evaluated). Focus group participants discuss their ideas and insights in response to open-ended questions from the facilitator. The strength of this method is that group discussion can provide ideas and stimulate memories with topics cascading as discussion occurs (Krueger et al., 2000; Morgan, 1997).

> The evaluation of community engagement may need both qualitative and quantitative methods because of the diversity of issues addressed

The strengths of qualitative data include providing contextual data to explain complex issues and complementing quantitative data by explaining the "why" and "how" behind the "what." The limitations of qualitative data for evaluation may include lack of generalizability, the time-consuming and costly nature of data collection, and the difficulty and complexity of data analysis and interpretation (Patton, 2002).

Mixed Methods

The evaluation of community engagement may need both qualitative and quantitative methods because of the diversity of issues addressed (e.g., population, type of project, and goals). The choice of methods should fit the need for the evaluation, its timeline, and available resources (Holland et al., 2005; Steckler et al., 1992).

EVALUATING THE COMMUNITY ENGAGEMENT PROCESS

In addition to ensuring that the community is engaged in the evaluation of a program, it is important to evaluate community engagement and its implementation. The purpose of this type of evaluation is to determine if the process of developing, implementing, and monitoring an intervention or program is indeed participatory in nature.

Questions to ask when evaluating community engagement include the following (CDC, 2009; Green et al., 1995; Israel et al., 1998):

- Are the right community members at the table? This is a question that needs to be reassessed throughout the program or intervention because the "right community members" might change over time.

- Does the process and structure of meetings allow for all voices to be heard and equally valued? For example, where do meetings take place, at what time of day or night, and who leads the meetings? What is the mechanism for decision-making or coming to consensus; how are conflicts handled?

- How are community members involved in developing the program or intervention? Did they help conceptualize the project, establish project goals, and develop or plan the project? How did community members help assure that the program or intervention is culturally sensitive?

- How are community members involved in implementing the program or intervention? Did they assist with the development of study materials or the implementation of project activities or provide space?

- How are community members involved in program evaluation or data analysis? Did they help interpret or synthesize conclusions? Did they help develop or disseminate materials? Are they coauthors on all publication or products?

- What kind of learning has occurred, for both the community and the academics? Have community members learned about evaluation or research methods? Have academics learned about the community health issues? Are there examples of co-learning?

As discussed in Chapter 6, social network analysis (SNA) is a mixed method that can be applied to the evaluation of community partnerships and community engagement (Freeman et al., 2006; Wasserman et al., 1994). This method looks at social relationships or connections and the strength of these connections. The relationships may be among a variety of entities, including people, institutions, and organizations. Methods that assess the linkages between people, activities, and locations are likely to be useful for understanding a community and its structure. SNA provides a set of tools for quantifying the connections between people based on ratings of similarity, frequency of interaction, or some other metric of interest. The resultant pattern of connections is displayed as a visual graphic of interacting entities depicting the interactions and their strength. Data for SNA may be collected through secondary (existing) sources or primary (new) sources, such as interviews and surveys. SNA is a useful approach to the evaluation of community partnerships and their sustainability as well as the impact of the partnership on community engagement (Wasserman et al., 1994). It is also useful in formative work to understand social networks and in planning and implementing organizational structures to facilitate community engagement initiatives as discussed in Chapter 4.

CHALLENGES

Engaging the community in developing and implementing a program evaluation can improve the quality and sustainability of the program. However, several challenges must be overcome to ensure an appropriate and effective evaluation. First, it is critical to have all stakeholders at the table from the conceptualization of the evaluation through implementation, analysis, and dissemination of the evaluation's results. Second, adequate organizational structures and resources are essential to engage the community in the evaluation, conduct it, and analyze and disseminate the results (see Chapter 4). Third, an evaluation that appropriately engages the community has the many benefits described in this chapter, but it takes more time than an evaluation conducted without community input. Fourth, different work styles and institutional cultures may make it difficult to develop or follow through on shared expectations or the meaningful reporting of results. Fifth, it is important that all persons involved understand that although the evaluation may identify problems and limitations that make them uncomfortable, addressing those issues can contribute to the program's improvement. Finally, an appropriate evaluation design and methodology should be used.

CONCLUSION

Program evaluation can take a variety of forms and serve a variety of purposes, ranging from helping to shape a program to learning lessons from its implementation or outcomes. Engaging stakeholders throughout the evaluation process improves the evaluation and positions these stakeholders to implement necessary changes as identified through the evaluation. Both participatory and empowerment evaluation are built on this insight and prescribe specific approaches to stakeholder involvement that are consistent with the principles of community engagement. Evaluating community-engaged partnerships in and of themselves is an emerging area. In addition, SNA and formal models of engagement may provide useful frameworks for evaluating engagement.

REFERENCES

Anderson RM, Funnell MM, Aikens JE, Krein SL, Fitzgerald JT, Nwankwo R, et al. Evaluating the efficacy of an empowerment-based self-management consultant intervention: results of a two-year randomized controlled trial. *Therapeutic Patient Education* 2009;1(1):3-11.

Burke B. Evaluating for a change: reflections on participatory methodology. *New Directions for Evaluation* 1998;(80):43-56.

Centers for Disease Control and Prevention. Framework for program evaluation in public health. *Morbidity and Mortality Weekly Report* 1999;48(RR11):1-40.

Centers for Disease Control and Prevention. *Prevention Research Centers: Evaluation results: Program context.* Atlanta (GA): Centers for Disease Control and Prevention; 2009. Retrieved from http://www.cdc.gov/prc/pdf/esfall2009-full.pdf.

Ericsson KA, Simon HA. *Protocol analysis.* Cambridge (MA): Massachusetts Institute of Technology; 1993.

Fetterman DM. Steps of empowerment evaluation: from California to Cape Town. *Evaluation and Program Planning* 1994;17(3):305-313.

Fetterman DM, Kaftarian SJ, Wandersman A. *Empowerment evaluation: knowledge and tools for self-assessment and accountability.* Thousand Oaks (CA): Sage; 1996.

Fetterman DM. Empowerment evaluation: *An introduction to process use.* 2008. Retrieved from http://www.rri.pdx.edu/fetterman_empowerment_10-2008.pdf.

Freeman J, Audia P. Community ecology and the sociology of organizations. *Sociology* 2006;32:145-169.

Garbarino S, Holland J. *Quantitative and qualitative methods in impact evaluation and measuring results.* Social Development Direct; 2009. Retrieved from http://www.gsdrc.org/docs/open/EIRS4.pdf.

Green LW, George MA, Daniel M, Frankish CJ, Herbert CP, Bowie WR, et al. *Study of participatory research in health promotion: review and recommendations for the development of participatory research in health promotion in Canada.* Ottawa, Canada: The Royal Society of Canada; 1995.

Holland J, Campbell J (editors). *Methods in development research: combining qualitative and quantitative approaches.* London, United Kingdom: ITDG Publications; 2005.

Israel BA, Shulz AJ, Parker EA, Becker AB. Review of community-based research: Assessing partnership approaches to improve public health. *Annual Review of Public Health* 1998;19:173-202.

Joint Committee on Standards for Educational Evaluation, Sanders J (editors). *The program evaluation standards: how to assess evaluations of educational programs* (2nd ed.). Thousand Oaks (CA): Sage; 1994.

Krueger R, Casey M. *Focus groups: a practical guide for applied research* (3rd ed.). Thousand Oaks (CA): Sage; 2000.

MacDonald G, Starr G, Schooley M, Yee SL, Klimowski K, Turner K. *Introduction to program evaluation for comprehensive tobacco control programs.* Atlanta (GA): Centers for Disease Control and Prevention; 2001.

Morgan D. *Focus groups and qualitative research.* Newbury Park (CA): Sage; 1997.

Mullan PB. Working to reduce maternal mortality in Sub-Saharan Africa: international fellowship program for Ghanaian physicians. *Medical Education at Michigan* 2009;5(2):16. Retrieved from http://www.med.umich.edu/meded/pdf/Newsletters/12-2009.pdf.

Parker E, Robins TG, Israel BA, Brakefield-Caldwell W, Edgren K, Wilkins D. Developing and implementing guidelines for dissemination. In: Israel BA, Eng E, Schulz AJ, Parker EA (editors). *Methods in community-based participatory research for health.* San Francisco: Jossey-Bass; 2005.

Patton MQ. *Qualitative evaluation and research methods.* Newbury Park (CA): Sage; 2002.

Patton MQ. *Utilization focused evaluation* (4th ed.). Saint Paul (MN): Sage; 2008.

Rossi P, Lipsey M, Freeman H. *Evaluation: a systemic approach* (7th ed.). Thousand Oaks (CA): Sage; 2004.

Steckler A, McLeroy KR, Goodman RM, Bird ST, McCormick L. Toward integrating qualitative and quantitative methods: an introduction. *Health Education Quarterly* 1992;19(1):1-8.

Wandersman A, Snell-Johns J, Lentz B, Fetterman D, Keener D, Livet M, et al. The principles of empowerment evaluation. *Empowerment Evaluation Principles in Practice* 2005;27-41.

Wasserman S, Faust K. *Social network analysis: methods and applications.* Cambridge, United Kingdom: Cambridge University; 1994.

Summary

Chapter 8
Summary

Donna Jo McCloskey, RN, PhD, and Mina Silberberg, PhD

This primer presents the case for community engagement in health promotion and research and provides guidelines for its practice. It emphasizes the need to articulate the purpose and goals of the engagement initiative, assess community capacity and one's own capacity for community engagement, and build or leverage community assets for health improvement. Community engagement, like any other initiative, needs to be implemented with a plan of action that is goal and context based. The stakeholders engaged, the strategy and approach used to gain their involvement, and the resources needed all depend on the purpose and outcomes desired and on knowledge of the community and the partners.

Community engagement may or may not be a new way of doing business for a given individual or entity. If it is new, it may mean changing the way organizations, individuals, and practices make decisions about programs and resource allocation. It may also mean developing partnerships, coalitions, and collaborative efforts with new people and organizations. Before action can occur, engagement leaders need to consider and develop a management strategy.

Assessing an organization's capacity for engaging the community involves looking at:

- The values of the organization: Does it perceive involving the community in identifying community health issues and developing programs as important? Does it recognize the importance of partnering and collaborating with other groups or community-based organizations?

- The intent of the organization: What does the organization want to accomplish? What is the best way to establish its position and select strategies to begin community action?

- The operations of the organization: Is it already working with the community on specific programs or issues? How? Are there existing collaborations with other institutions or agencies? Are community leaders or representatives already involved in decision making related to program planning, implementation, and evaluation?

- The resources and expertise available to support an engagement effort: What mechanisms will be in place to ensure that relevant data on community needs will be used? What financial resources will be required? Which staff are most skilled or already have strong ties to the community?

In articulating the purposes or goals of a community engagement effort, there is value in thinking through a few key issues:

- Know what is of interest and what community involvement is expected to accomplish. For example, is the goal a broad one, such as engaging the community in assessing its health status, identifying concerns, and developing and implementing action plans, or is it more narrow, such as engaging the community around specific health objectives?

- Have an idea about how the community should be involved. Will they be advisors or co-decision makers or both? What might the structures and process be for their involvement?

- Be clear on the community to be engaged, at least initially. Is it a geographic community, including all of those who live within its boundaries, or is it a community that is defined in some other way?

- Know the extent to which the focus of the community engagement efforts is flexible. As more is learned about the community and issues of interest, it might be more effective or appropriate to focus engagement efforts on other populations or communities. Similarly, goals may need to be modified based on community input.

Finally, to learn about communities, you must:

- Talk with stakeholders, attend community meetings, read community newspapers, and obtain information that is relevant to the engagement process.

- Establish relationships and build trust.

Potential partners will be more likely to become involved in a community engagement effort, such as collaborative health promotion or research projects, if they understand what it means to become involved and believe their participation will be meaningful. Using a community-engaged approach and working within communities requires a continual effort to balance costs and benefits and sustain cooperation and accountability among participating groups. All interested individuals, groups, and organizations must feel they can join a community engagement effort and influence it. This is the foundation for trust among collaborators. If trust is not present, relationships are guarded and commitments tentative. Therefore, relationships must be built that are inclusive of the entire community of interest.

> All interested individuals, groups, and organizations must feel they can join a community engagement effort and influence it.

Being inclusive can create some organizing challenges. However, successfully overcoming these challenges will provide a greater return on the investment made by engagement leaders through the greater involvement of partners and the assets they bring to the process. One key challenge is managing the decision-making process. When formal governance of the collaboration is needed, the community should be given an opportunity to shape the governance process and provide input on decisions to be made by the governing structure. Another important approach to creating and maintaining a sense that participation is worthwhile is to use collaborative strategies that can achieve a small success quickly and reinforce the benefit of participation. With time, collaborations may evolve from these "small beginnings" and grow into more ambitious efforts. Over time, it may be appropriate for an entity to move away from a position as a lead stakeholder to become simply one of many partners in a broader effort. In addition, stakeholders may find that they no longer need to reach out to involve a community because that community is now coming to them. Over time, engagement leaders may also need to reexamine and revise the purpose, goals, and strategies of the collaborative. Engagement leaders may find that it is time to broaden the participation and engage new communities on new issues while nurturing existing collaborations.

CONCLUSION

The contributors to this second edition of Principles of Community Engagement hope that it will provide all stakeholders with greater insight into the science and practice of community engagement and the implementation of community-engaged initiatives. These insights should help prepare those interested in community engagement to practice in the diverse situations that communities face. Most importantly, the insights provided in this primer should help prepare engagement leaders to make decisions that improve health, reduce disparities, and enhance quality of life.

Appendix A:

Acronyms

APPENDIX A: ACRONYMS

AAHIP   African-American Health Improvement Partnership

ACE   Active Community Engagement

ACQUIRE   Access, Quality and Use in Reproductive Health

AHRQ   Agency for Healthcare Research and Quality

ALA   American Lung Association

AME   African Methodist Episcopal

ATSDR   Agency for Toxic Substances and Disease Registry

CAB   community advisory board

CAC   community advisory committee

CACHÉ   Community Action for Child Health Equity

CAN DO   Children And Neighbors Defeat Obesity/la Comunidad Ayudando a los Niños a Derrotar la Obesidad

CARE   Community Alliance for Research and Engagement

CBO   community-based organization

CBPR   community-based participatory research

CCAT   community coalition action theory

CCB   Community Coalition Board

CCHN   Community Child Health Network

CDC	Centers for Disease Control and Prevention
CEnR	community-engaged research
CHC	Community Health Coalition
CHIC	Community Health Improvement Collaborative
CTSA	Clinical and Translational Science Awards
DCCR	Duke Center for Community Research
DCH	Division of Community Health
DEPLOY	Diabetes Education & Prevention with a Lifestyle Intervention Offered at the YMCA
DPBRN	Dental Practice-Based Research Network
DPP	Diabetes Prevention Program
HAAF	Healthy African American Families
HHP	Hispanic Health Project
HOC	Healing of the Canoe
HWA	Houston Wellness Association
IRB	institutional review board
IUSM	Indiana University School of Medicine
JABGC	John Avery Boys and Girls Club
JHCC	Joyland-Highpoint Community Coalition
MOA	memorandum of agreement

MUSC	Medical University of South Carolina
MWC	Mayor's Wellness Council
NCCU	North Carolina Central University
NICHD	National Institute of Child Health and Human Development
NIH	National Institutes of Health
N-O-T	Not on Tobacco
NPU-Y	Neighborhood Planning Unit Y
PA	physical activity
PBR	practice-based research
PBRN	practice-based research network
PI	principal investigator
PRC	Prevention Research Center
RCT	randomized controlled trial
SCC	Suquamish Cultural Cooperative
SNA	social network analysis
SuGAR	Sea Island Genetic African American Registry
UCLA	University of California, Los Angeles